邯郸名物

SKETCHES OF CLASSIC HANDAN

汪 芳 田 潇 文　Written by Wang Fang and Tian Xiao
徐翔宇 刘天羽 绘　Illustrated by Xu Xiangyu and Liu Tianyu
马 睿 译　Translated by Ma Rui

中国画报出版社·北京
China Pictorial Press·Beijing

图书在版编目（CIP）数据

邯郸名物：汉英对照 / 汪芳，田潇文；徐翔宇，
刘天羽绘；马睿译. -- 北京：中国画报出版社，2025.
9. -- ISBN 978-7-5146-2582-0

Ⅰ. K292.23

中国国家版本馆CIP数据核字第2025R795L4号

邯郸名物（汉英对照）

汪芳　田潇　文　　徐翔宇　刘天羽　绘　　马睿　译

出 版 人：方允仲
策划编辑：刘晓雪
特约作者：李晓玲　范文华
责任编辑：王韵如
艺术顾问：荆　鹏
英文编辑：牛语晨
英文改稿：埃尔维斯·安伯
英文定稿：蒋雪飞
封面设计：王建东
内文排版：赵艳超
责任印制：焦　洋

出版发行：中国画报出版社
地　　址：中国北京市海淀区车公庄西路33号　邮编：100048
发 行 部：010-88417418　010-68414683（传真）
总编室兼传真：010-88417359　版权部：010-88417359

开　　本：16开（787mm×1092mm）
印　　张：15
字　　数：200千字
版　　次：2025年9月第1版　2025年9月第1次印刷
印　　刷：北京汇瑞嘉合文化发展有限公司
书　　号：ISBN 978-7-5146-2582-0
定　　价：118.00元

序言

　　邯郸之名，起于"甘丹"。日出东方的赤色平川，落日如墨的太行余脉，明月高挂的滏阳之河，描绘出它壮美的山河天际。

　　邯郸，从殷商小邑到赵国国都，从此声名鹊起，几度盛极而衰，衰极而起；屡次败而后兴，兴而愈盛，直至今日。回首凝望，它是华夏文明的微缩史诗——磁山文化的石镰翻开了农耕序章，胡服骑射的铁骑踏出了变革强音，古邺城中轴线之美演绎着中国古代都城的营建典范，响堂山石窟文化闪耀着驼铃丝路之光……这片土地的厚重与智慧，熔铸出不可复制的文化基因。1959年9月，毛泽东主席视察邯郸时指出"邯郸是赵国的都城，是五大古都之一……邯郸是要复兴的……"。邯郸人民在这一伟大号召鼓舞下，披肝沥胆、砥砺奋进，让梦想一步步走向现实。时至今日，一个崭新的邯郸再次屹立在新时代的冀南大地上。

　　邯郸，正以古今交响演绎着复兴新篇。邯郸道上，重振丛台鼓，复燃紫宫灯，抟心揖志，铸其风骨，再拓山河又一程。回车巷口，当年礼让成佳传，今作潮街聚人愿，可谓时空交错，一城双面，月照千年真梦幻。成语方特，全息复

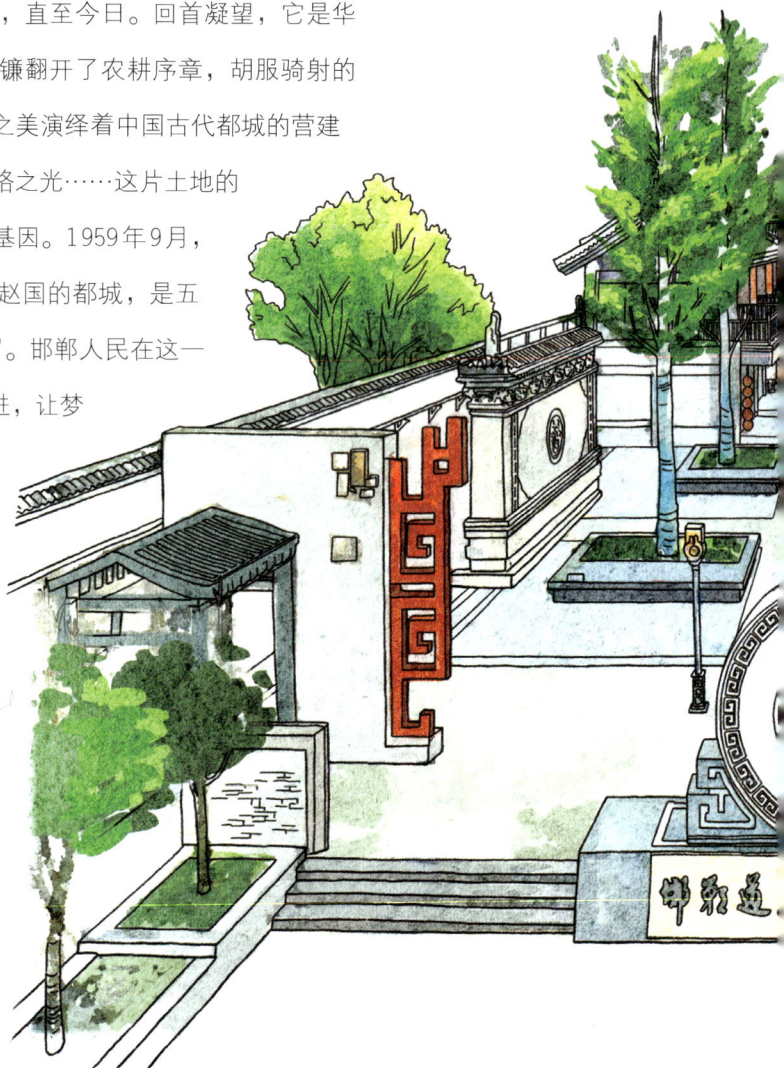

Foreword

The name Handan finds its origin in "Gandan." Crimson plains where the sun rises in the east, the ink-dark ridgelines of the Taihang Mountains at dusk, and the Fuyang River gleaming beneath a full moon—together, they sketch a magnificent panorama of its landscape and skies.

From a small settlement during the late Shang Dynasty to the capital of the State of Zhao, Handan has risen to prominence, flourishing time and again through cycles of prosperity and decline. Again and again, it has rose fiercer from each fall, growing ever more vibrant into the present day. Looking back, Handan is like a miniature epic of Chinese civilization: stone sickles from the Cishan culture turned the first pages of agrarian history; the mounted warriors clad in *hufu* during the era of Wearing *hufu* (costumes of nomads) and Practicing Mounted Archery sounded the call for reform and strength; the central axis of ancient Yecheng city showcased a model of ancient capital planning in China; and the Xiangtangshan Grotto Complex glowed with the radiance of Silk Road caravans and the jingling of camel bells. The depth and wisdom of this land have forged an irreplaceable cultural DNA. In September 1959, during his inspection of Handan, Chairman Mao Zedong declared: "Handan

活，千年典故焕新容，转瞬间唐宋相逢。广府城中，百年传道远，五洲弟子，阴阳双鱼转，寰宇此式同……

邯郸，这一条可触摸的"时空走廊"，它的每一块城砖、每一段老墙，都是活着的历史剧本；每一座古桥、每一条街巷，皆是跨时空的舞台剧场。它们就像漫天星光，你我懂得仰望，才知其辽阔。

太多太多的邯郸故事，想要告诉你。故而，我们用画笔与轻阅读方式，还原这些名物的温度。手绘线条勾勒出的不仅是地理形胜，更是邯郸人的待客之心。浅白文字解读的不仅是本土风物，更是城市文明的基因密码。这一切，触手可感；这一切，皆为"时间的胶囊"，治愈你与邯郸之间的三千年时差。

当你踏上这片土地时，我们为你浅唱低吟"既见君子，云胡不喜""我有嘉宾，鼓瑟吹笙"……

was the capital of the State of Zhao, one of the five great ancient capitals... Handan must be revitalized..." Inspired by this grand call, the people of Handan poured their hearts into tireless effort, step by step turning dreams into reality. Today, a renewed Handan stands tall once more upon the land of southern Hebei, embracing the new era.

Handan is now composing a new chapter of revival through a symphony of past and present. On Handandao, the drums of Congtai are sounding again, the lanterns of the Purple Palace relit. With unwavering spirit and heartfelt determination, the city's character is being reforged, its reach across rivers and mountains extending yet again. At the mouth of Huiche Lane, where once courtesy became legend, a vibrant modern street now gathers crowds and wishes. Here, time intertwines: one city, two faces, and a moonlit dream that has endured for millennia. At the Idiom-themed Fantawild and the Holographic Revival attractions, ancient Chinese tales and sayings are brought to life in new and vivid forms. Blink, and the Tang and Song dynasties seem to meet again. In Guangfu Ancient City, generations have passed down teachings to disciples from across the globe; the swirling yin-yang fish in Tai Chi draw the world together in one shared form...

Handan is a tangible "corridor through time." Each brick in its walls, each segment of its ancient streets, is a living script of history. Every old bridge and winding alley is a stage set for cross-temporal theater. They are like stars scattered across the sky. You only need to look up to understand their vastness.

There are so many stories Handan longs to tell you—so many invitations it wishes to extend. That is why we've chosen to portray these iconic elements through hand-drawn illustrations and light, accessible reading. The lines we sketch capture not only the city's geography but also the warmth with which Handan welcomes its guests. The simple prose does more than explain local customs. It reveals the genetic code of the city's civilization. All of this is within reach; all of this is a "time capsule" to bridge the 3,000-year gap between you and Handan.

As you set foot on this land, we softly sing for you: "Now that I have seen the gentleman, how could I not rejoice?" "With honored guests, we shall strike the zither and play the flute..."

目录
Contents

序言
Foreword

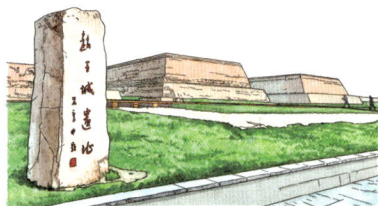

第二章 Chapter 2

千年历史会客厅
A Reception Hall of Millennia

第四章 Chapter 4

赵都古建拼图
The Architectural Puzzle of the Zhao Capital

第五章 Chapter 5

红色能量补给站
A Red Spirit Revival Station

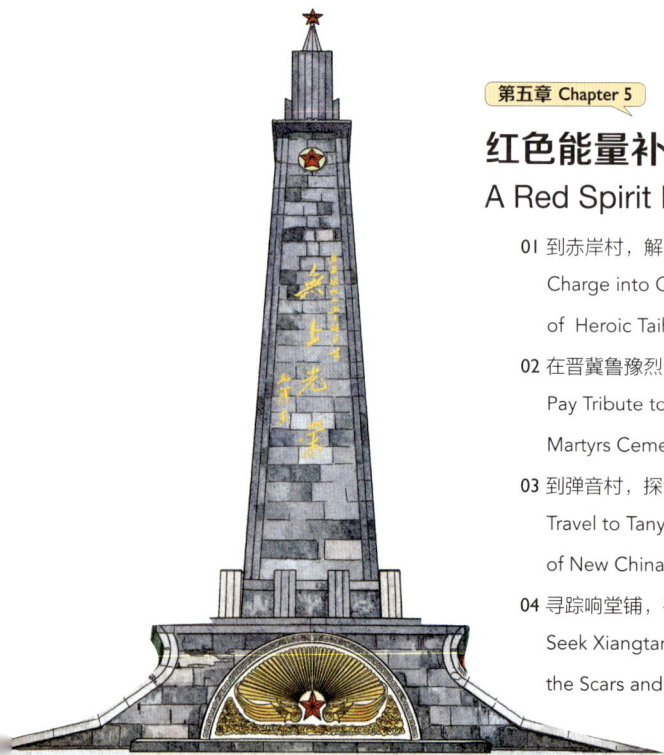

一口吃掉三千年
A Bite Through Three Thousand Years

百里青峦见悠然
Where Endless Peaks Cradle Unhurried Joy

千年古城变形记
The Metamorphosis of a Millennia-Old City

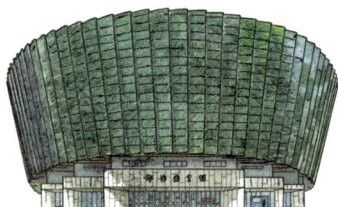

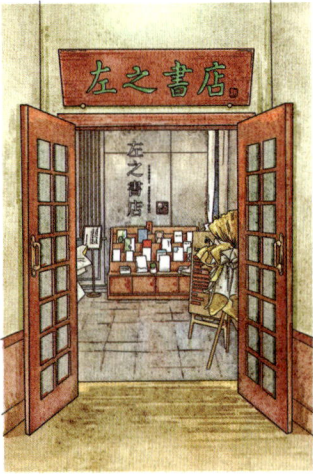

　　以时间轴为经，文物遗址为纬，邯郸从史前文明到明清时期的完整历史脉络和文化谱系缓缓铺开，呈现这座城市作为"华夏文明核心现场"的八千年演进史。

　　This chapter weaves a chronological narrative using historical relics and archaeological sites to present the complete historical development and cultural lineage of Handan—from prehistoric civilization through the Ming and Qing dynasties—unveiling its eight-thousand -year evolution as a "core site of Chinese civilization."

与邯郸对酌三千年

A Toast to Three Thousand Years of Handan

丛台区人民东路 399 号文化艺术中心西侧 · No. 399 East Renmin Road,
west side of the Handan Cultural and Arts Center, Congtai District

漫步邯郸市博物馆，探寻"甘丹"风华
Stroll Through the Handan Museum to Discover the Elegance of "Gandan"

"邯郸"作为城市名称最早出现在殷商后期，此后三千多年未曾更改。当我们走入邯郸市博物馆，那些青铜器上的斑驳铭文、陶器上的古老纹饰，都在无声诉说着这座城市跨越三千个春秋的等待。作为国家一级博物馆，这里馆藏文物近万件（套），以新石器时代早期磁山文化遗址文物、先商文物、赵国文物等最具特色。

令人震撼的是那三匹战国青铜马——比"马踏飞燕"还早四百年的写实杰作，仿佛随时会冲破历史的禁锢，带着两千多年前的战火硝烟奔腾而来。而那尊被称为"邯郸微笑"的唐代红砂石罗汉造像，其永恒的笑容让人觉得邯郸的魅力就在于这种穿越时空的友善与温和。

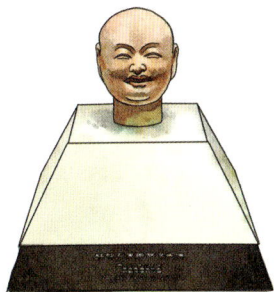

The name "Handan" first appeared in the late Shang Dynasty (1600–1046 BC) and has remained unchanged for over 3,000 years. As we step into the Handan Museum, the weathered inscriptions on bronze vessels and the ancient patterns on pottery seem to silently narrate the city's long wait spanning three millennia. As a national first-class museum, the Handan Museum houses nearly 10,000 cultural relics (including sets), with its most distinctive collections being artifacts from the early Neolithic Cishan culture site, pre-Shang relics, and cultural treasures from the State of Zhao.

The most breathtaking exhibit is a group of three bronze horses of the Warring States Period (475–221 BC)—realistic masterpieces predating the famed "Flying Horse of Gansu" by 400 years. They seem poised to break through the confines of history, galloping forth with the smoke and fire of war from over two millennia ago. Nearby, a Tang Dynasty (618–907) red sandstone Arhat statue known as the "Handan Smile" bears an eternal grin—suggesting that Handan's charm lies in this gentle and friendly spirit that transcends time.

武安市 206 县道与普陀湖观音道场东南 · Southeast of the intersection of County Road 206 and Putuo Lake Guanyin Bodhimanda, Wu'an City

来中国磁山文化遗址博物馆，体验八千年前的远古生活
Step Back Eight Thousand Years to Experience the Dawn of Civilization at Cishan Culture Site Museum

在考古研究中，鸡骨遗骸为家鸡豢养起源提供了关键证据，碳化核桃推翻了学界关于核桃系汉代张骞出使西域带回的传统认知。而作为这些文物的发现地，磁山文化遗址，距今已有八千多年历史，其发掘填补了我国新石器时代考古研究的空白，为探索中华文明源头提供了宝贵资料。

这座以磁山文化为主题的博物馆，是展示中华文明早期足迹的重要窗口。步入展馆，四根神鸟图腾柱撑起了这片远古的天空，十三米高的中华文明源浮雕墙铺开了历史的画卷。最令人眼前一亮的是，博物馆通过声光电等现代技术，展现了古代版"李子柒"们的生活日常：搭房子，养鸡，带娃，狩猎，用陶盂和鸟头形支脚做饭。来都来了，可

千万别错过"磁山人家"展区——置身其中，仿佛穿越回远古时代，还能跟那时的街坊邻里打个照面。

In archaeological research, chicken bone remains have provided key evidence for the domestication of chickens, while carbonized walnut shells have overturned the long-held belief that walnuts were introduced to China during the Han Dynasty (206 BC–AD 220) via Zhang Qian (164–114 BC)'s expedition to the Western Regions. These findings originate from the Cishan culture site, which dates back over 8,000 years. Its excavation filled a gap in China's Neolithic archaeology and provided invaluable materials for tracing the origins of Chinese civilization.

This museum, themed around the Cishan culture, serves as a vital window into the early footprints of Chinese civilization. Upon entering, four divine bird totem columns uphold the ancient sky, while a 13-meter-high bas-relief wall unfolds the grand tapestry of history. Most striking is how the museum uses sound, light, and other modern technology to present the daily life of ancient counterparts to modern DIY creators like Li Ziqi: building shelters, raising chickens, caring for children, hunting, and cooking with pottery basins and bird-headed tripod supports. Don't leave without visiting the "Cishan Family" exhibit—standing there, it feels as if you've traveled back to ancient times, even brushing shoulders with neighbors from 8,000 years ago.

03

逛邯郸道，探寻两千年历史文脉
Wander Handandao, Tracing Two Thousand Years of History

　　李白的"把酒顾美人，请歌邯郸词"，叹年华易逝，应及时行乐；岑参的"客从长安来，驰马邯郸道"恣意潇洒又畅快淋漓。漫步邯郸道，不仅能体验战国雄风、北朝风云、唐宋运河、太极神韵、红色风华，还能在荀子学堂、李白的邯郸、赵女馆等场馆感受邯郸的文化精髓。邯郸道见证了古赵国的兴衰，聆听过先秦诸子的众声鼎沸，品味过唐宋文人的诗酒风流。而那汉文帝高歌、慎夫人鼓瑟的悠扬乐声依旧在此地回荡，悠悠不绝。

　　明清时期，太保张国彦在此留下"忠直"足迹，贞元增烧坊酿就的美酒曾飘香宫廷。如今，邯郸道已从历史深处华丽转身，古朴建筑与现代商业交织，传统文化与科技生活共舞，形成一种"现代脚步丈量历史长廊"的独特魅力！而其中采用"战汉"式仿古设计的过街天桥，成了游客们争相拍照打卡的"网红桥"。走在桥上，仿佛你我也曾在三千年前擦肩而过。

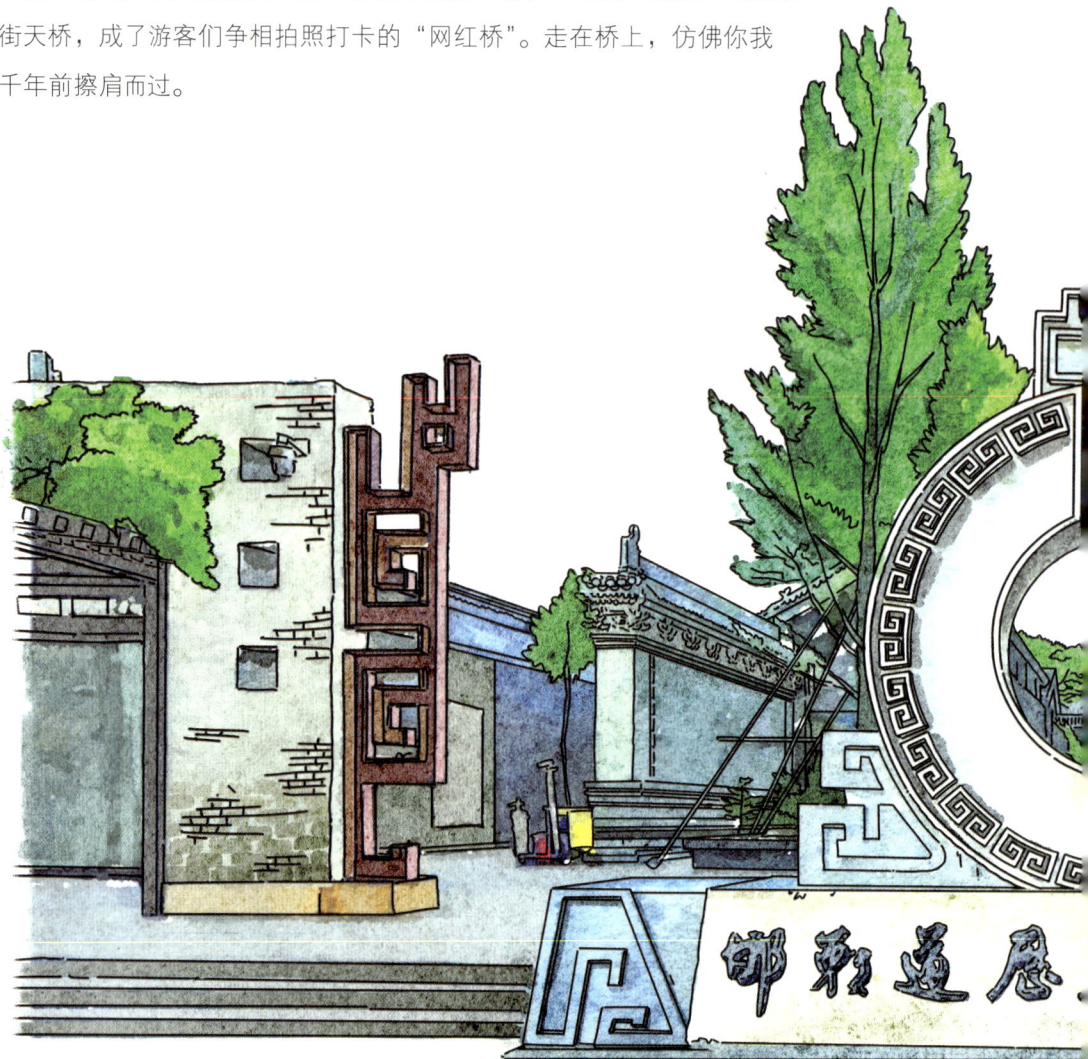

Li Bai (701–762) once wrote, "With wine in hand, I invite the beauty to sing songs of Handan," lamenting fleeting youth and urging indulgence in the moment; Cen Shen wrote, "A guest comes from Chang'an, galloping down the Handan road," a carefree and exhilarating journey. Walking along Handandao, a historical and cultural district, offers not only glimpses of the Warring States Period's glory, upheavals of the Northern Dynasties (439–581), the Tang and Song (960–1279) canal cultures, the spirit of Tai Chi, and red cultural heritage, but also immersive experiences at venues such as the Xunzi School, Li Bai's Handan, and the Ancient Zhao Heroines Hall. It has witnessed the rise and fall of the ancient State of Zhao, echoed with the debates of pre-Qin thinkers, and savored the poetic elegance of Tang and Song literati. The melodious tunes sung by Emperor Wen of Han (203–157 BC) and strummed by Consort Shen still seem to linger in the air.

During the Ming (1368–1644) and Qing (1644–1911) dynasties, Zhang Guoyan (1525–1598), Grand Tutor to the Crown Prince, left behind a legacy of loyalty and integrity here, and the fine liquor brewed at Zhenyuanzeng Distillery once graced the imperial courts. Today, Handandao has been magnificently transformed from a relic of the past. Rustic architecture intertwines with modern commerce, traditional culture dances with technology-driven lifestyles, creating a unique allure where modern footsteps traverse a historic corridor. A street bridge designed in the "Warring States–Han" retro style has even become an Internet-famous spot—walk across it, and you might feel as though you've brushed past someone from 3,000 years ago.

04

逛学步桥，感悟成语真谛
Visit the Xuebu Bridge to Understand the True Meaning of a Chinese Idiom

　　在邯郸道北端，始建于明代的多孔梁桥，以生动的建筑语言诠释着"邯郸学步"这一经典成语故事。当年寿陵少年在此偷师邯郸人走路，结果"未得国能，又失其故行矣"的名场面，被庄周写成《秋水》顶流梗。如今学步桥上人潮汹涌，却不知哪一步照应了几千年前的姿势。

　　学步桥下碧水悠悠，倒映着当年踉跄学步者的身影。细看栏板浮雕，胡服骑射的利落与学步者的笨拙同框，堪称古代行为艺术展。当夕阳泼洒在学步桥上，耳边传来的不再是学步者身旁围观者的忍俊不禁，而是这两千多年时过境迁，岁月静好的幸福欢笑，而学步者的故事也成为了邯郸重要的文化符号，吸引了无数游客来欣赏邯郸人的走姿。

At the northern end of Handandao stands a multi-arch beam bridge built during the Ming Dynasty, vividly illustrating the classic idiom "Learning to Walk in Handan" through architectural storytelling. Long ago, a youth from Shouling came here to imitate the Handan's famed walking style, only to end up "failing to learn the new and forgetting the old." This iconic blunder was immortalized by Zhuangzi in his "Autumn Floods" chapter. Today, the Xuebu Bridge is bustling with crowds—yet no one knows whose stride mirrors that of a youth from millennia past.

Beneath the bridge, the serene green waters reflect the clumsy figure of that long-ago learner. Take a closer look at the balustrade's bas-reliefs: the contrast between the sharp, confident figure in *hufu* (costumes of nomads) practicing mounted archery and the awkward mimic is like a gallery of ancient performance art. As the setting sun bathes Xuebu Bridge in golden light, the chuckles of onlookers fade, replaced by the peaceful laughter of a life transformed by time. The youth's story has become a cultural symbol of Handan, drawing countless visitors to admire the famed Handan walk.

05

丛台区丛台西街道中华北大街 159 号丛台公园内 · In Congtai Park, No. 159 Zhonghua North Street, Congtai West Subdistrict, Congtai District

登武灵丛台，触摸战国雄风的历史脉动
Climb the Wuling Congtai and Touch the Historical Pulse of Warring States Grandeur

欲知邯郸，先登丛台！武灵丛台据考证始建于战国赵武灵王赵雍时期，是赵王检阅军队与观赏歌舞之地。颜师古《汉书注》称，因楼榭台阁众多而"连聚非一"，故名"丛台"。两千三百年前，赵武灵王以短袍紧裤取代宽袍大袖，既打造了精锐之师，又引领了时代风尚。这里不仅是军事改革的核心现场，更是引领列国潮流的时尚中心；东汉刘秀丛台置酒，开创光武盛世；盛唐李白在此豪情落笔："歌酣易水动，鼓震丛台倾"；乾隆皇帝也不禁感叹："丛台下，渭桥边，豪华瞥眼二千年。"望着斑驳的砖石，便会明白为何武灵丛台能成为邯郸的象征：它不仅是建筑遗存，更是一个民族勇于变革的精神图腾。

萧瑟的秋风吹过武灵丛台，拂过七贤祠，掠过望诸榭，擦过石碑林，浸润着从简牍书卷中带来的千古哲思。

To understand Handan, one must first climb Congtai! Historical records confirm that the Wuling Congtai was first built during the reign of King Wuling of Zhao, Zhao Yong (?–295 BC), in the Warring States Period. It served as a platform where the king reviewed troops and enjoyed musical performances. *Annotations to the Book of Han* by Yan Shigu (581–645) notes that the site was named "Congtai" (literally in Chinese meaning "clustered terrace") due to the many pavilions and towers densely assembled there. Over 2,300 years ago, King Wuling of Zhao replaced flowing robes with short tunics and tight trousers, creating an elite army and setting a fashion trend that swept through the states. This was not only the core site of military reform but also the fashion center that influenced an entire era. During the

Eastern Han (25–220), Emperor Liu Xiu (5 BC–AD 57) held banquets here, marking the beginning of the prosperous Guangwu reign. In the flourishing Tang, poet Li Bai wrote with great flair: "As the singing stirs the Yishui River, the drums shake Congtai." Even Emperor Qianlong (1711–1799) couldn't help but marvel: "Beneath Congtai, beside Wei Bridge—splendor in a fleeting glance spans two thousand years." Gazing upon the weathered stones of Congtai, one begins to understand why this site has become a symbol of Handan. It's not just a historical structure, but a spiritual totem of a people's courage to embrace change.

As the autumn wind sweeps through Wuling Congtai, brushing past the Shrine of the Seven Sages, the Wangzhu Pavilion, and the forest of stone steles, it carries with it ancient philosophical wisdom echoing from bamboo slips and scrolls across millennia.

06

邯山区西环与南环交叉口北侧 · North side of the intersection of West Ring and South Ring Roads, Hanshan District

在赵王城国家考古遗址公园，来一场战国风"角色扮演"
Play a Warring States Role at Zhao King City National Archaeological Site Park

当微风扬起战国袍的衣角，信步踏上东边的龙台，恍惚间似与往昔相遇——这不是幻境，而是21世纪的赵王城国家考古遗址公园。它拥有同时代最完整、最大规模的遗址，是我们追忆战国的最佳地点。

向西走去，进入赵王城遗址博物馆，这里通过历史遗产与现代科技的结合，重现了这座古都的盛世风华。馆内陈列的珍贵文物，都在诉说着"从前有座城……"的传奇。

漫步过那幅巨大的《赵都赋》，感受着古赵王城遗址的一砖一瓦，或许那阵扬起衣角的风，也来自几千年前。

When the breeze lifts the hem of your Warring States robe, and your steps carry you to the eastern Dragon Terrace, you may feel as if you've met the past—this is no illusion, but the Zhao King City National Archaeological Site Park of the 21st century. It is the most complete and largest site of its time, making it the perfect setting for remembering the Warring States era.

Head west to the Zhao King City Site Museum, where historical heritage is brought to life through modern technology, recreating the ancient capital's former splendor. Inside, precious cultural relics tell the legendary tale of "Once upon a time, there was a city…"

Stroll past the giant bas-relief, depicting *Zhao Capital Rhapsody*, and as you take in every brick and tile of the ancient Zhao capital site, perhaps that gust of wind that lifted your robe also came from thousands of years ago.

07

丛台区联纺路桥西 200 米 · 200 meters west of Lianfang Road Bridge, Congtai District

来赵苑公园，试一下战国版"美颜相机"
Try the Warring States "Beauty Filter" at Zhaoyuan Park

嘿！赵苑公园可不是普通公园！这里绿意盎然不说，还是赵武灵王搞"军事改革"的核心现场。当年"胡服骑射"的创新壮举，在插箭岭这片土地上留下了不朽的印记。

可如果你觉得这里只有骑射嘶风的武灵王，那就错了。园内的照眉池，那水面简直就是古代宫女的"美颜相机"，波光粼粼中仿佛还能看到古代"小仙女"们对着池水描眉画眼的可爱模样。诗仙李白的"清虚一鉴湛天光，曾照邯郸宫女妆"也不是随便说说的，那可是最强"种草笔记"！这里还有九宫听香、妆台梳云的典雅，茅沼消夏、林樾宿芳的清凉，等等。景区将生态与人文交织融合，营造出这一片既能够休闲娱乐，又可感受历史文化的精神家园。

Hey! Zhaoyuan Park is no ordinary park! Beyond its lush greenery, it was the core site of King Wuling of Zhao's "military reform." His bold initiative—wearing *hufu* and practicing mounted archery—left an indelible mark right here on the land of Chajian Ridge.

But if you think it's all galloping horses and military drills here, think again. Inside the park lies Zhaomei Pool, whose shimmering surface was practically the "beauty filter" of the ancient palace maids. In the rippling water, you can almost see graceful "little fairies" of old delicately drawing their eyebrows and applying makeup. Li Bai, the immortal poet, once wrote, "The pure mirror reflects heavenly light—it once illuminated the palace maids of Handan." That wasn't just poetic flair—it's the ultimate historical "influencer recommendation!" You'll also find elegant sites like "Fragrance Echoes through the Nine Pavilions" and "Clouds Combed at the Dressing Terrace," and refreshing retreats like "Summer Retreat at the Reed Marsh" and "Fragrant Dreams Beneath Shaded Groves." Blending ecological beauty with cultural depth, this park is more than a place for rest and recreation—it is a spiritual haven where visitors can experience both leisure and the living essence of history.

08

临漳县北堤路与漳河北大堤交叉口正北方向 41 米 · 41 meters due north of the intersection of Beidi Road and Zhanghe River North Embankment, Linzhang County

在邺城国家考古遗址公园，历史变得触手可及
Let History Come Alive at Yecheng National Archaeological Site Park

被誉为"三国故地、六朝古都"的邺城，如今以国家考古遗址公园的姿态向我们展开怀抱。踏上铜雀台，仿佛真的能看到曹操与文臣武将开怀痛饮，觥筹交错。

邺城国家考古遗址公园宛如一本立体的历史书，将三国至隋唐的辉煌文明娓娓道来，东魏北齐宫城区的考古发掘现场更是让历史变得触手可及。这里不仅记录着文明的脚步，更是文化的活水。在公园内的邺城博物馆，那些令人爱不释手的文创产品——铜雀瓦砚、文武杯、邺城萌娃等，每一件都凝聚着邺城的文化精髓，都是邺城的文化符号，是数千年前历史的回响。

Once praised as the "land of the Three Kingdoms and ancient capital of six dynasties," Yecheng now welcomes us in the form of a National Archaeological Site Park. Standing atop the Bronze Sparrow Terrace, you can almost see the legendary scenes of Cao Cao feasting and drinking with his civil and military officials.

The Yecheng National Archaeological Site Park reads like a three-dimensional history book, vividly recounting the glory of the Three Kingdoms Period (220–280) through the Sui (581–618) and Tang dynasties. The archaeological site of the palace district from the Eastern Wei (534–550) and Northern Qi (550–557) dynasties makes history feel within reach. This park not only records the steps of civilization—it is a living stream of culture. At the Yecheng Museum located within the site, you'll find irresistible cultural creations like Bronze Sparrow-style tile inkstones, literary and martial cups, and adorable Yecheng mascots. Each item encapsulates the essence of Yecheng's cultural identity, standing as a symbol of the city and echoing the spirit of its millennia-old past.

09

磁县和谐大道与 G107 交叉口西北侧 900 米 · 900 meters northwest of the intersection of Hexie Avenue and G107, Cixian County

在北朝考古博物馆，见证"东西方文化大联欢"的精彩现场
Witness the East-West Cultural Spectacle at the Northern Dynasties Archaeological Museum

这个藏在深山人未识的"文化宝库"，珍藏了东魏、北齐出土的诸多珍贵文物，记录了千年前的民族融合和东西方文明的碰撞。

馆内陈列的珍贵文物，每一件都诉说着东魏北齐的传奇历史。东罗马帝国的金币与丝路商队的陶骆驼，带领我们重回丝绸之路；汉族、鲜卑族、西域人的陶俑群像，将那个海纳百川、兼容并蓄的盛世图景永恒定格。精美绝伦的湾漳壁画，以其卓越的艺术造诣，彰显着北朝时期壁画艺术的巅峰成就，实为一场艺术的盛宴。尤为珍贵的是茹茹公主墓志铭，不仅为补充《资治通鉴》的记载提供了证据，更让茹茹公主的故事跃然眼前——她的喜怒哀乐、荣辱沉浮，正透过斑驳的字迹向我们娓娓道来……

Hidden deep in the mountains, this "cultural treasure trove" houses numerous precious artifacts unearthed from the Eastern Wei and Northern Qi dynasties—bearing witness to the ethnic integration and civilizational fusion between East and West a thousand years ago.

Each relic on display tells a legendary tale of the Eastern Wei and Northern Qi dynasties. Byzantine gold coins and pottery camels from Silk Road caravans take us back to the heart of the Silk Road. Figurines of Han, Xianbei, and Western Region peoples capture forever the grandeur of an inclusive and harmonious golden age. The exquisite Wanzhang murals, outstanding in both artistry and execution, stand as a peak achievement of mural art in the Northern Dynasties, truly a visual feast. Especially noteworthy is the epitaph of Princess Ruru (537–550), which not only provides evidence supplementing the *Historical Events Retold as a Mirror for Government*, but also vividly brings to life the princess's joys and sorrows, her triumphs and tribulations—softly narrated through the weathered inscriptions.

大名县大名府路与京府大街交叉口东正南方向 190 米 · 190 meters due south
of the intersection of Damingfu Road and Jingfu Street, Daming County

久闻大名，打卡北宋"水浒朋友圈"
Famous for a Thousand Years, Check in with the Northern Song's "Water Margin Circle of Friends"

"一部水浒传天下，世人皆知大名府。"这座低调了千年的北宋陪都之一———北京大名府，可是藏着东京开封府《清明上河图》的番外篇。

大名古城，城垣巍然，四门古朴，建筑宏伟，犹见当年雄姿。古城墙是华北罕见的明代军事遗存，斑驳的墙砖见证着这里的沧海桑田、岁月变迁。步入其间，扑面而来的是满满的历史感与生活气息。古城里的街巷，再现了大名市集曾经的模样，古今交错间，历史不再是课本上方正沉默的汉字，而是化身为可打卡的非遗店铺与可体验的"宋式"烟火气。

暮色渐浓时，登临城墙远眺，夜市如昼，俯瞰墙下，游人熙攘，恍然穿越回《水浒传》中那个"赛挂好灯，巧样烟火；各设灯火，庆贺丰年"的花好月圆之夜。

"The world knows Daming Prefecture from the tale of the *Water Margin*." One of the lesser-known co-capitals of the Northern Song Dynasty, the Northern Capital, Daming Prefecture, has quietly stood for a thousand years. It serves as a supplement to *Along the River During the Qingming Festival*, the iconic scroll

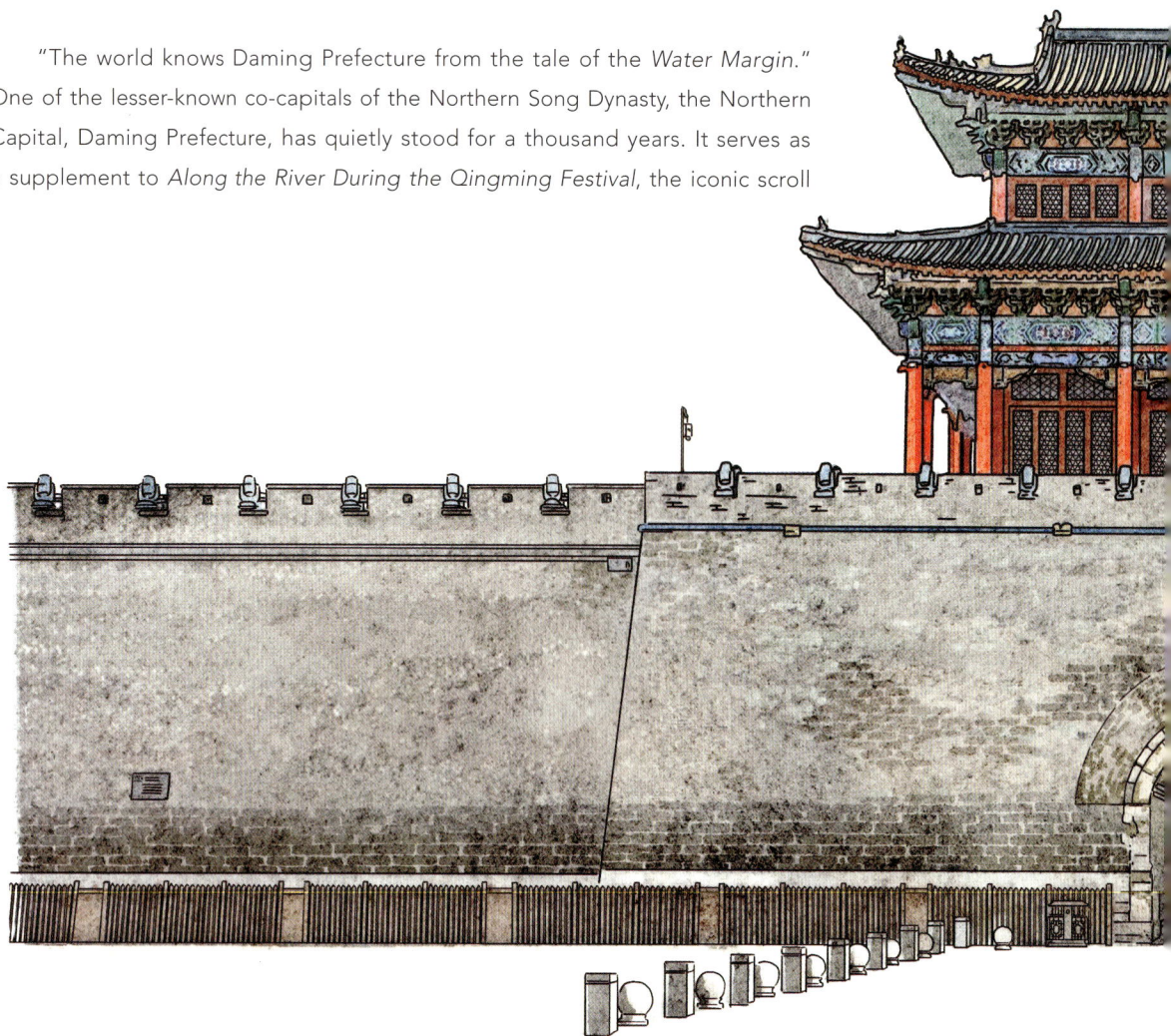

painting set in the Eastern Capital (Bianliang, present-day Kaifeng), the main capital of the Song Dynasty.

The ancient city of Daming stands tall with its grand architecture and dignified city gates— its towering walls a rare surviving military relic from the Ming Dynasty (1368–1644) in North China. Weathered bricks bear witness to centuries of change. Step inside and you're immediately immersed in both deep history and the vibrancy of everyday life. The alleys and markets bring to life the bustling Daming of the past. Here, history is no longer rigid textbook characters. It has transformed into intangible heritage shops you can visit and Song-style "street life" experiences you can live.

As dusk deepens, climb the city walls and gaze into the distance—the night market glows like daytime. Looking down, crowds swirl and music fills the air, transporting you back to that unforgettable *Water Margin* scene: "Lanterns hung like constellations, fireworks bursting in artful display; lights adorned every corner to welcome a bountiful year."

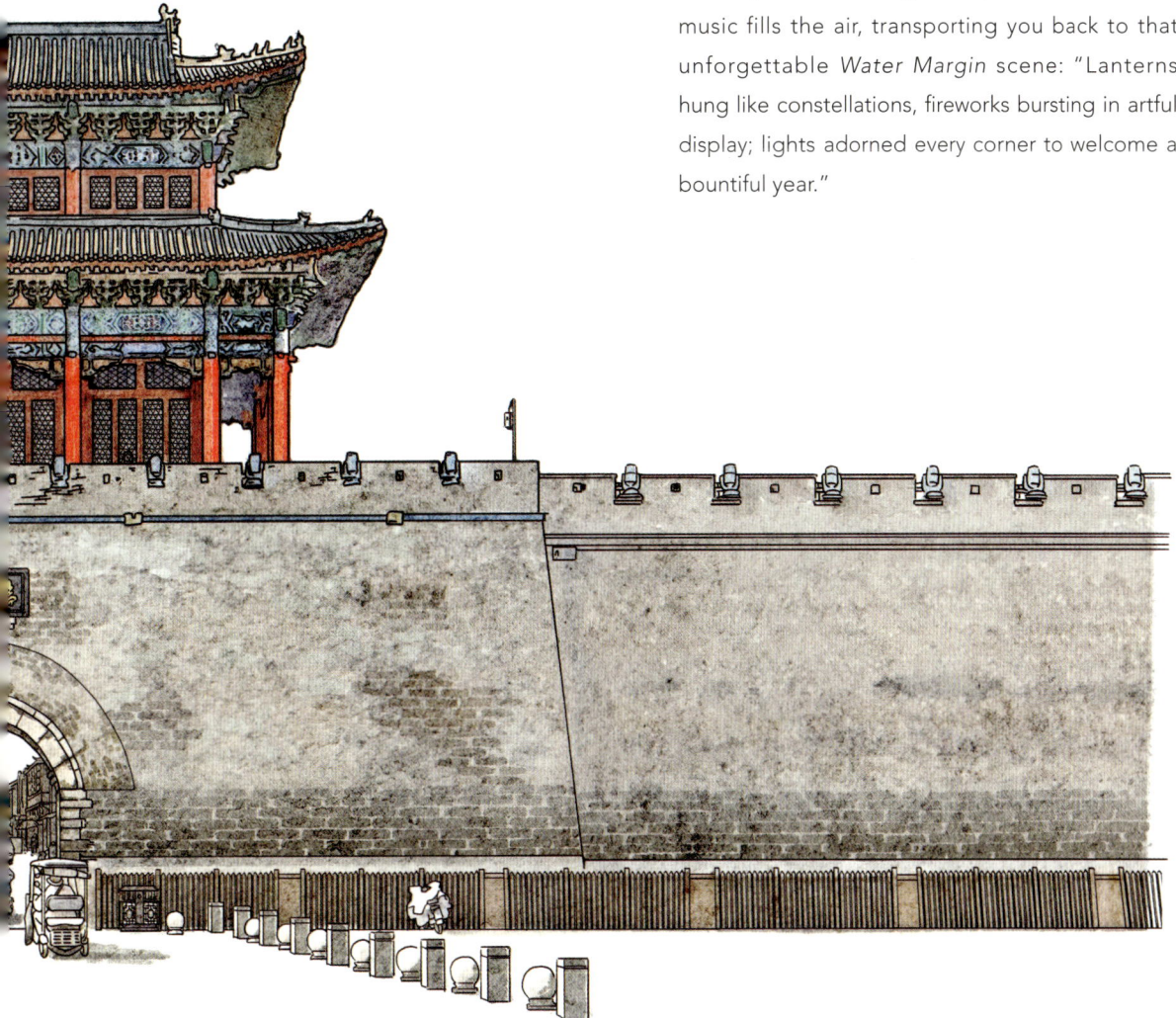

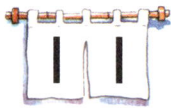

永年区邯临路与人民路旅游专线交叉口北 20 米路东 · 20 meters north of the intersection of Hanlin Road and Renmin Road Tourist Line, east side of the road, Yongnian District

在"北国小江南"的氤氲中，打一套太极拳
Practice Tai Chi Amid the Misty Charm of "Little Jiangnan of the North"

　　车近广府，景致渐开——古城沧桑的轮廓、洼淀的碧波与太极的灵韵尽入眼帘。万顷湿地如明镜镶嵌在大地上，环抱着一千四百多年岁月沉淀的广府古城，水面荷花竞放，粉白相间；轻舟划过，涟漪惊起的水鸟，振开金色的羽翼。这般景致，果然不负"北国小江南"盛名。

　　清晨薄雾中，可见白发老者在城墙上演练太极拳，衣袂翻飞如白鹤亮翅。这里是杨氏、武氏太极拳的发源地，连街边卖烧饼的大爷都能来段"云手"。随着太极拳最后一式的收招，抬头可见始建于隋朝的广府古城墙与天边流云相接。向北望去，广平府署上的"公生明"三字熠熠生辉；向南看去，城边的杨露禅故居、迎春街上的武禹襄故居，依然留存着大师们的生活印记。信步前行，不觉已至甘露寺前——这座饱经战乱的古寺，当地人用虔诚的信仰将其一遍遍修复，它们不再是冰冷的石头，而是中华民族不可磨灭的记忆的延续。

As your car approaches Guangfu, the scenery begins to unfold—ancient city outlines, shimmering wetland waters, and the graceful rhythm of Tai Chi come into view. Tens of thousands of acres of wetlands, like a mirror set into the earth, encircle Guangfu Ancient City, which bears over 1,400 years of history. Lotus blossoms bloom across the water, pink and white; boats glide by, startling waterfowl into golden-winged flight. Such beauty lives up to the name "Little Jiangnan of the North."

On misty mornings, white-haired elders can be seen on the city walls practicing Tai Chi—their flowing sleeves like cranes in flight. This is the birthplace of both Yang-style and Wu-style Tai Chi. Even the baked bun vendors on the street can demonstrate a few moves of "Cloud Hands." As the final Tai Chi posture settles into stillness, you look up to see the ancient Guangfu city walls, first built in the Sui Dynasty, merging into drifting clouds on the horizon. Looking north, the words "Justice Gives Rise to Clarity" shine from the Guangping Prefecture office. Looking south, the former residences of Yang Luchan (1796–1872) and Wu Yuxiang (1812–1880), masters of the art, still stand on Chengbian and Yingchun Streets, quietly preserving their legacy. Wandering forward, you soon arrive at Ganlu Temple, this war-scarred ancient temple has been lovingly restored time and again by the devotion of the locals who transformed cold stone into vessels carrying the indomitable memory of our Chinese civilization.

　　邯郸就像一间"历史会客厅"，拥有多元文化交汇地的特质，众多耳熟能详的历史人物在邯郸留下了"双向奔赴"故事：将相之和的政治智慧、以柔克刚的太极文化、浪漫潇洒的建安风骨与依法治国的法治精神，以及贯穿邯郸古今的发展变革精神。邯郸的宴席永不散场，此刻，您的席位已在历史与未来之间备妥——请品鉴这杯用三千年光阴酿造的邯郸故事。

　　Handan stands as a "reception hall of history," where civilizations converged and great historical figures left timeless stories of mutual pursuit. It reflects the political wisdom of "The General and the Minister Reconciled," the soft-overcomes-hard philosophy of Tai Chi, the romantic and unrestrained spirit of the Jian'an era, the legalist ideals of governing by law, and a spirit of reform that has guided Handan from ancient times into the present. The banquet of Handan never ends—and now, your seat is ready, set between past and future. Come savor this cup of Handan's story, brewed over three thousand years.

千年历史

会客厅

Chapter Two: A Reception Hall of Millennia

丛台区城内中街 12 号甲 4 号 · No. 12 Jia-4, Chengnei Middle Street, Congtai District

去回车巷，直击战国第一会车现场
Step Into Huiche Lane to Witness the First Chariot Standoff of the Warring States Period

导航提示：前方道路狭窄，建议回车——这不是系统故障，而是穿越千年的"战国版智慧导航"正在为您指路！在这仅有 2.3 米宽的巷子里，数千年前上演了蔺相如为廉颇回车让路的佳话。看似寻常的巷陌，却因"将相和"的典故而流芳千古，这条窄巷不仅成就了邯郸史上一段"和衷共济"的佳话，更铸就了邯郸城内"以和为贵"的城市品格。

如今的巷子早已盛满了岁月静好的人间烟火，可每当风穿过砖缝，仍会漏出战国的马车擦过墙壁的颤音——那个遥远的午后，蔺相如和廉颇在此不期而遇。黄昏时分，更适合打卡回车巷，当斜阳把巷子拉成一道时光隧道，漫步其间，可以沉浸式体验那场改写赵国命运的"倒车入库"。

Navigation alert: "Narrow road ahead, U-turn recommended"—this isn't a system error, but a "Warring States Edition" smart navigation guiding you across time! In this alley just 2.3 meters wide, the legendary moment when Lin Xiangru yielded his chariot to Lian Po unfolded thousands of years ago. At first glance, it's just another ordinary alley—but because of the timeless tale of "The General and the Minister Reconciled," it has become immortal in history. This narrow lane not only witnessed one of the greatest stories of mutual understanding in Handan's history, but also forged the city's lasting civic character of "harmony above all."

Today, the alley brims with the warmth of everyday life. Yet when the wind whistles through the cracks in the bricks, it still carries the trembling echo of chariots brushing past ancient walls. On that distant afternoon, Lin Xiangru and Lian Po met unexpectedly right here. Dusk is the perfect time to explore Huiche Alley. As the slanting sun stretches the alley into a tunnel of time, stroll through Huiche Lane and immerse yourself in the Warring States-style "parking maneuver" that changed the destiny of the State of Zhao.

02

到礼贤台，学习魏文侯的顶配人才政策
Climb Lixian Terrace to Witness Marquis Wen of Wei's Elite Recruitment Strategy

　　河北魏县东北角，藏着一座"战国人才市场"——礼贤台。战国时期著名"人事经理"魏文侯在此网罗天下人才，就算是之前翻墙逃避见面的清高的段干木，也被魏文侯扶轼致敬的真诚所打动，铸就了"干木富义"的佳话。自此，魏国跃居战国七雄之首，开创了一代盛世。

　　如今重建的二十六米高台，坐拥"一湖一台一河一湾"的神仙布局：西揽漳河湾碧波，南抱墨池湖烟雨，湖中梨花仙子雕像与杜郎隔水相望，似在演绎着"舍肉救母"的千年传说。当夜色落幕，击掌石阶，回音如鸟鸣春涧，恍惚撞见文侯正对段干木长揖："先生，魏国就靠你了！"此刻脚下不再是死板的土石草木，而是邯郸人敬才爱才的精神具现。

In the northeastern corner of Weixian County, Hebei, lies a "Warring States-period talent marketplace"—Lixian Terrace. Here, the famed "HR manager" of the Warring States, Marquis Wen of Wei, gathered the finest minds of the age. Even the proud Duangan Mu (c. 475–396 BC), who once climbed over a wall to avoid meeting him, was ultimately moved by the Marquis's sincerity, standing by his carriage in respectful greeting, and together they created the legendary tale of "The Righteous Duangan Mu." From then on, the Wei State rose to the top among the Seven Warring States, ushering in an age of glory.

The rebuilt terrace, now 26 meters high, boasts an ethereal setting of "one lake, one terrace, one river, one bay." To the west, it overlooks the clear waters of the Zhanghe River bend; to the south, it embraces the misty landscapes of Mochi Lake. In the lake, a statue of the pear-blossom fairy faces Duanlang across the water—as if silently reenacting the ancient tale of sacrificing flesh to save one's mother. As dusk falls, strike the stone steps and the echoes ripple like birdsong in a springtime stream. In that moment, it's as if Marquis Wen is bowing deeply to Duangan Mu: "Sir, the State of Wei now rests in your hands!" What lies beneath your feet is no longer mere earth and stone—it is the spirit of Handan's reverence for talent, brought vividly to life.

03

去紫山风景区，寻根问祖、追古溯今
Trace the Root and Unearth the Past in Zishan Scenic Area

在武灵丛台的一方刻石上，镌刻着胡景翼先生题写的八个大字"滏流东渐，紫气西来"，前者描绘了蜿蜒东去的滏阳河，后者叙述的便是邯郸的紫山。紫山巍峨静立，是邯郸的一抹紫色灵韵，素有"邯郸第一山"之誉。暮色西沉时，落日余晖洒在紫山的紫英石上，折射进城内，形成独特的霞光奇观，这也是邯郸人独有的"紫气西来"。紫山，这个浸润着神秘紫光的风景名胜，还暗藏着一段赵姓与马氏的历史渊源——马氏源于赵姓，其始祖是战国时代的"执法硬汉"——赵奢。如今，赵奢墓庄重肃穆地伫立在紫山半腰，成为马氏宗族寻根问祖的圣地。

此外，人文底蕴深厚的紫山，更孕育了无数文化硕果，元代理学大家刘秉忠在此创办紫山书院，培育出郭守敬等"紫山五杰"。如今的紫山公园，绿树成荫，紫云湖碧波荡漾，在生态修复工程的"美颜滤镜"下焕然一新，成为传统与现代完美融合的"打卡胜地"！

On a carved stone beside Wuling Congtai, several bold characters inscribed by Mr. Hu Jingyi read: "The Fuyang River flows east, auspicious purple comes from the west." The first describes the meandering Fuyang River; the second tells the story of Handan's Zishan Mountain. The Zishan Mountain stands tall and serene, a purple-hued spiritual beacon of Handan, long regarded as "Handan's First Mountain." At sunset, golden light falls upon the mountain's purple quartz, casting a glow across the city and creating the unique spectacle known to locals as "auspicious purple comes from the west." This scenic landmark bathed in mystical light also carries the intertwined histories of the Zhao surname and the Ma clan. The Ma family traces its roots to the Zhao line, and their founding ancestor was Zhao She—a fearless enforcer of justice in the Warring States Period. Today, Zhao She's solemn and dignified burial mound still stands halfway up Zishan, a sacred site for the Ma clan's ancestral pilgrimages.

Zishan's cultural legacy runs deep, giving birth to countless cultural achievements. During the Yuan Dynasty (1279–1368), Neo-Confucian master Liu Bingzhong (1216–1274) established the Zishan Academy here, nurturing scholars like Guo Shoujing (1231–1316)—one of the celebrated "Five Talents of Zishan." Today, Zishan Park is shaded by lush trees, its Ziyun Lake rippling in the breeze. Thanks to ecological restoration projects, the park has been beautifully renewed—now a "must-visit site" where tradition and modernity blend in perfect harmony.

04

刷秦始皇出生地纪念馆，围观千古一帝的童年片场

Visit the Birthplace Memorial of Emperor Qin Shi Huang to Witness the Childhood of the "OG Hero"

提到邯郸就不得不回忆起古赵国，提到赵国就不能不想到秦始皇嬴政。邯郸丛台公园西南部，一座灰砖青瓦的纪念馆，便可带您复盘这千古一帝的初始局。

馆前小径蜿蜒，灰砖青石间镌刻着"易守难攻""背水一战"等典故。窗棂内嵌玄鸟图腾，象征着秦赵同源。馆内的铜版浮雕中，秦始皇雄姿勃发，帝王气度跃然眼前。

别小看了那些在邯郸经历的时光，它开拓了少年秦始皇的视野与志向。或许正是在这里，他萌生了统一天下的宏伟梦想，埋下了后来变法图强的种子。想象一下，当年那个在邯郸街头玩耍的小男孩，竟然真的成为名冠古今、驰名中外的千古一帝，是不是超级励志？

When we speak of Handan, we cannot help but recall the ancient State of Zhao—and when we speak of Zhao, we must think of Emperor Qin Shi Huang (259–210 BC). In the southwest corner of Handan's Congtai Park, a gray-bricked, blue-tiled memorial hall retraces the earliest chapter of this "First Emperor of the Ages."

The winding path leading to the hall is etched with phrases like "easy to defend, hard to attack" and "fight with one's back to the river." Inlaid within the window lattices is the mysterious *xuan niao* (literally "dark bird" in Chinese) totem, symbolizing the shared ancestral origins of the Qin and Zhao peoples. Inside, copper bas-reliefs depict the majestic figure of Qin Shi Huang, his imperial presence leaping vividly to life.

Never underestimate the time young Qin Shi Huang spent in Handan—it broadened his vision and forged his ambition. Perhaps it was here that the seeds of his dream to unify the realm were first planted, the beginning of his later reforms and rise to strength. Imagine that little boy once playing on the streets of Handan, who would one day become a name that echoes through history—now that's what you call truly inspirational.

秦始皇出生地纪念馆

05

漫步毛遂文化园，重温战国时代的"自荐传奇"
Stroll Through the Mao Sui Cultural Park and Relive a Legendary Warring States "Job Interview"

古人不懂得"自我营销"？不，战国外交家毛遂会让你大开眼界。在那个风云变幻的年代，平原君府邸内，群贤荟萃，却见一位名不见经传之人从容而出，自信开口道："臣乃今日请处囊中耳。"这不禁让人感叹：好一个"求职达人"，这份不卑不亢的态度，更引得后人争相效仿，这次求职表现，也称得上古代最高能的面试现场。

步入园中，首先映入眼帘的是国内最大的单体毛遂雕像，塑像手按长剑，面带自信，展现了毛遂勇于自荐、敢于担当的精神和赴楚合纵、气吞云梦的气势。而在文化园的西北边，是与毛遂息息相关的毛氏宗祠，毛氏宗祠内有一块刻有"鸡泽韶山毛氏一家亲"字样的纪念石刻，与韶山毛泽东纪念园的"鸡泽韶山毛氏一家亲"纪念石刻一模一样，石刻背后的骈文形象地叙述了鸡泽韶山毛氏血脉相连的故事，两块石刻可谓"姊妹石"。

Think ancient people didn't know how to market themselves? Think again. The Warring States diplomat Mao Sui will blow your mind. In that turbulent era, within the residence of Lord Pingyuan, the most brilliant minds of the day had gathered—when suddenly, a previously unknown figure stepped forward and calmly declared: "I am the sword in your sheath, ready to be drawn today." One cannot help but admire this master of self-recommendation—his poised and confident demeanor sparked admiration through the ages, making this one of the most legendary "interview scenes" in all of Chinese history.

As you enter the park, the first thing to greet your eyes is the largest standalone statue of Mao Sui in China. Hand resting on his long sword and face brimming with confidence, the statue captures Mao Sui's bold spirit of volunteering and courageously taking on great responsibility—as well as the imposing aura he brought to his diplomatic mission in Chu, where he "swallowed the clouds of Yunmeng Lake." In the park's northwest corner stands the ancestral temple of the Mao clan, closely tied to Mao Sui's legacy. Inside, a commemorative stone engraved with the phrase "One Family, Mao Clan of Jize and Shaoshan" mirrors an identical inscription found at the Mao Zedong Memorial Garden in Shaoshan. The carved prose on the back tells the story of the bloodline shared between the Mao clans of Jize and Shaoshan, making these two stones true "sister monuments."

三台胜境

曹操

登铜雀三台，参观曹操的"顶级秀场"
Climb the Bronze Bird Terraces to Visit Cao Cao's Ultimate "Showground"

河北临漳县深藏着三国政治家曹操的"诗与远方"——铜雀三台遗址。金凤、铜雀、冰井，这三座漳河畔的"天际线"，是曹操的顶级秀场：铜雀台宴饮赋诗，金凤台运筹帷幄，冰井台藏冰储粮。这里是曹操集权、文治、享乐的超级综合体。

三台之中，铜雀台最负盛名。曹操当年登台设宴，邀群臣子弟共赋新篇。曹植挥毫写下"愿斯台之永固兮，乐终古而未央"的瑰丽诗篇。唐代诗人杜牧更以"东风不与周郎便，铜雀春深锁二乔"之句，为此台平添几分浪漫遐思。千年文脉在此交汇，终将此地的人文气象推向巅峰。

In Linzhang County, Hebei, lies a hidden gem—the Bronze Bird Terraces, a place that embodies the poetic aspirations and grand ambitions of Cao Cao (155–220), a famed politician of the Three Kingdoms Period. The three platforms—Golden Phoenix, Bronze Sparrow, and Ice Well—once formed the skyline along the Zhanghe River, serving as Cao Cao's ultimate showground. The Bronze Sparrow Terrace was for feasting and composing poetry; the Golden Phoenix Terrace for strategic planning; and the Ice Well Terrace stored ice and grain, functioning as an "ancient refrigerator." Together, they formed a super complex of political power, cultural sophistication, and elite indulgence.

Among the three, the Bronze Sparrow Terrace gained the greatest renown. In Cao Cao's day, he ascended the terrace, hosted grand banquets, and composed verse with his ministers and sons. Cao Zhi (192–232) penned the dazzling line, "May this terrace last forever, and joy endure throughout the ages." Later, the Tang poet Du Mu (803–852) added a touch of romance with his famous line: "Had the east wind not favored Zhou Yu, the two Qiao sisters would now be locked deep in the Bronze Sparrow in spring." Centuries of literary brilliance converge here, elevating this site to the pinnacle of cultural prestige.

磁县 147 乡道与环村路交叉口东北 240 米 · 240 meters northeast of the intersection of Township Road 147 and Huancun Road, Cixian County

07

访兰陵王墓，听《入阵曲》，感受忠魂壮烈
Visit the Tomb of the Prince of Lanling to Hear the Heroic Echo of *The Battle Song*

听说过"音容兼美"的战神吗？战场上戴着"凶神恶煞"面具冲锋陷阵，摘下面具却是一位妥妥的"男神"。认识一下，他便是"北齐第一猛将"兰陵王高长恭！

他生得清雅如玉，眉目如画，偏偏生逢乱世，只得将俊美容颜藏于狰狞面具之下，披甲执锐，纵马沙场。史载邙山一战，他率五百铁骑破敌十万，铁蹄踏碎烽烟，长戟挑落残阳。凯旋时，将士们击节而歌，遂成《兰陵王入阵曲》，其声慷慨激越，听之让人振奋不已、情怀激荡。

如今他的墓冢静静矗立着，精致的透花围墙、庄重的碑亭，沉淀着战神的传奇故事，也叹息着他的悲怆终局。邯郸磁县的土地之下，千百年后依旧回响着高长恭爱国的心跳声。邙山的风沙，终将"忠以事上，和以待下"八个字吹成血色的叹息。

Ever heard of a war god who was both a beauty and a beast? Meet Gao Changgong (541–573), the Prince of Lanling! This "number one general of Northern Qi" charged into battle wearing a fierce demon mask—but beneath it was the face of a true "male idol."

Elegant as jade and striking as a painting, he was born into a chaotic era where his beautiful face had to be hidden behind a terrifying mask. Clad in armor and wielding his spear, he galloped into battle like a tempest. Records say that at the Battle of Mangshan, he led 500 cavalry to crush an enemy force of 100,000—iron hooves smashing through the flames of war, his halberd piercing the setting sun. Upon his victorious return, the soldiers burst into song, creating the legendary *The Prince of Lanling Enters the Battle*. Stirring and fierce, the anthem still rouses hearts to this day.

Today, his tomb stands in solemn silence, encircled by a finely carved lattice wall and a stately stele pavilion—each element bearing witness to the war god's heroic saga and lamenting his tragic end. Beneath the earth of Cixian County in Handan, the heartbeat of patriotist Gao Changgong still echoes through the ages. As the wind sweeps the sands of Mangshan Mountain, it carries the blood-stained sigh of the eight words he lived by: "Serve with loyalty above, treat with harmony below."

08

故居新游，体验太极宗师的"平行宇宙"
Take a New Tour on Old Homes to Experience the "Parallel Universe" of Tai Chi Grandmasters

"太极生两仪，两仪生四象，四象生八卦。"永年广府城里的两处故居，一砖一瓦都彰显着邯郸"太极之乡"的美誉。邯郸作为太极拳的发源地之一，其刚柔并济、天人合一的文化精髓也深入邯郸人心中。

南门处，杨露禅故居静立于此。传言道：杨宗师昔日只是推车贩煤的少年，凭借对武艺的执着追求，从药铺掌柜处习得一招绝技，由此开启了"三下陈家沟"的传奇篇章，成为享誉全国的太极宗师。

东门旁，武禹襄故居庄重雅致。这座清代大院，曾是一位文人潜心研究武学的净土。武禹襄在此精研太极、著述《太极拳解》。据说，院中那两棵石榴树，一酸一甜，恰似太极阴阳，相生相济。

"From Tai Chi arise the two modes, from two modes come the four forms, and from four forms emerge the eight trigrams." In Guangfu Ancient City, Yongnian District, Handan, two former residences stand as quiet testaments to why this place is hailed as the "Hometown of Tai Chi." As one of the birthplaces of Tai Chi, Handan has fully absorbed its essence—balancing softness with strength, uniting humanity with nature—and embedded it deep into the local spirit.

At the southern gate lies the Former Residence of Yang Luchan, standing in silent reverence. Legend has it that Yang, once a humble coal vendor pushing a cart, gained a secret self-defense technique from a pharmacy owner, launching his legendary "three visits to Chenjiagou Village." His relentless effort finally made him a Tai Chi grandmaster known throughout the nation.

At the eastern gate, the Former Residence of Wu Yuxiang exudes an air of quiet elegance. This Qing Dynasty courtyard was once the scholarly sanctuary of a man devoted to martial arts study. Here, Wu immersed himself in Tai Chi and authored the *Explanation of Tai Chi*. It's said that two pomegranate trees grow in the courtyard—one sour, one sweet—perfectly mirroring the yin-yang philosophy of Tai Chi, where opposites coexist and complement each other.

09

大名县从峰线与园中街交叉路口往东约 130 米・About 130 meters east from the intersection of Congfeng Line and Yuanzhong Street, Daming County

摸一把狄仁杰祠堂碑，解码狄公的另一面
Touch the Stele at Di Renjie's Shrine to Uncover Another Side of Lord Di

提到狄仁杰，你是不是想到了那句经典台词："元芳，你怎么看？"不过比起断案如神，他留给历史的更多的还是大公无私，一心为民的贤臣形象。

邯郸大名孔庄村，青石巨碑半截扎进黄土，见证着这位清官的传奇历史。武则天万岁通天年间，契丹压境，魏州刺史狄仁杰以"万一贼来，吾自当之"的胆识及过人智慧，竟让契丹自动退兵，化解了危机！魏州人连夜建造生祠，将这份敬重与感激之情具象化，让后人时刻谨记这位贤臣能臣的事迹。这块石碑不仅记录了狄仁杰的政绩，更体现了他"天下为公"的政治理念。

如今，篆额"大唐狄梁公祠堂之碑"仍透着魏州人对狄公诉说不尽的尊敬与崇拜。冯宿之文的忠义报国、胡证笔锋里的颜体风骨、田弘正重建祠堂的夯土声，全被封印铸刻在这段岁月中。

Mention Di Renjie (630–700) and you might instantly recall the famous catchphrase: "Yuanfang, what do you think?" But the legacy of this legendary Tang Dynasty official goes far beyond detective skills—he is remembered as a selfless, devoted statesman who governed with the people at heart.

In Kongzhuang Village, Daming County, Handan, a massive bluestone stele is half-buried in loess soil, bearing witness to the legacy of this incorruptible official. During Empress Wu Zetian's Wansui Tongtian era (696–697), as the Khitans threatened the borders, Di Renjie, then governor of Weizhou (today's Daming County), declared, "If the enemies come, I shall face them myself!" His bravery and sharp intellect caused the Khitans to retreat without a fight, averting the crisis. In gratitude, the people of Weizhou erected a shrine overnight to immortalize their admiration and respect—ensuring that future generations would remember this virtuous and capable official.

The stele records not only his accomplishments, but also his political ideal of "governing for the common people."

Today, the inscription "Stele of the Ancestral Shrine of Lord Di of the Great Tang" still radiates the profound respect and reverence Weizhou's people held for Di Renjie. Feng Su (767–836)'s tribute to loyal service, Hu Zheng (758–828)'s brush echoing the strength of Yan-style calligraphy, and Tian Hongzheng (764–821)'s rammed-earth rebuild are all sealed and carved into this enduring chapter of history.

10

望胡服骑射铜像，忆赵国改革新风
Look upon the "Wearing Hufu and Practicing Mounted Archery" Bronze Statue to Recall the Reformist Spirit of the State of Zhao

在邯郸东环路与邯临公路交叉口，一尊二十四米高的铜像霸气侧漏——赵武灵王骑在马上，穿着胡服，披风扬起，似要张弓搭箭，展现出一代雄主的气魄与远见。这不仅是邯郸的"城市名片"，更是古代版"改革开放"的超前教科书！

两千三百多年前，赵国被邻居们欺负得很惨，赵武灵王决定"升级装备"，开创了中原文化与塞外文明交融的先河。他借鉴外族的生活习惯，扔掉雍容华贵的长袍，换上便捷利落、便于骑马射箭的胡服。这波"带货"太有效，国民纷纷效仿，自此赵国军事实力显著提升。

如今铜像中战马前蹄高扬，仿佛要踏破古今。有意思的是赵王手里有弓无箭——据说这是设计师的小心机，引来无数游客脑洞大开。最有可能的解读便是，如今已经是和平盛世，不再提倡好战的品行，武器更多用作震慑邪恶，守卫和平。

At the intersection of Donghuan Road and the Hanlin Highway in Handan, a towering 24-meter-tall bronze statue dominates the landscape. It depicts King Wuling of Zhao riding a horse, dressed in *hufu* and draped in a billowing cloak, ready to draw his bow—radiating the determination and foresight of a visionary ruler. This is more than a landmark—it's Handan's signature image and an ancient masterclass in "reform and opening-up."

Over 2,300 years ago, the State of Zhao was repeatedly attacked by its neighbors. King Wuling boldly decided to "upgrade the gear" and pioneered a fusion of Central Plains and nomadic cultures. He adopted the lifestyle of foreign peoples, ditching the ornate but impractical robes for *hufu*—functional attire suited for horseback archery. His hands-on reform campaign was a roaring success—citizens followed his lead, Zhao's military might skyrocketed, and the state quickly rose to power.

The statue's rearing horse seems ready to leap across the ages. Most intriguing is the bow in the king's hand—without an arrow. Some say it's a clever design twist, sparking endless speculation among visitors. The most likely interpretation is that we now live in an era of peace, where belligerence is no longer glorified, and weapons serve more as a deterrent to evil than a call to war.

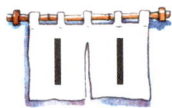

广平县广安东路与长春大道南段交叉口西南角中央公园内，Southwest corner inside Central Park, intersection of Guang'an East Road and South Segment of Changchun Avenue, Guangping County

观葛鹅雕塑，感受战国女性高光时刻
Gaze at the Ge E Sculpture to Celebrate a Warring States Woman's Highlight

自古邯郸出美女，如独立自信的秦罗敷，才貌无双的蔡文姬，美艳绝伦的貂蝉，还有赵姬、慎夫人……但广平城有一位奇女子，她不仅美，还很飒。

七米高的青铜战马上，一位女子迎风而立，长剑破空，英气逼人，仿佛从两千年前的烽烟中策马而来——她，正是赵武灵王的王后葛鹅。这位传奇女子率先穿胡服、挽强弓，更亲自督建"赵南长城"最东段，自此，"葛鹅城"成了广平的千年代号。赵武灵王与葛鹅这对"事业型搭档"用实际行动证明：最好的爱情是并肩"革新"。

黄昏，青铜战马的鬃毛被晚霞镀上一层柔和的金光，这份静谧的光影交错，犹如千年岁月凝结的记忆。鹅城女将筑城戍边的壮举永远铭刻在广平人民心中，成为世代传颂的巾帼传奇。这座雕塑，正是对这位巾帼英雄的崇敬与怀念。

Handan has long been known for its beautiful women—from the poised and confident Qin Luofu, to the brilliant and talented Cai Wenji, to the breathtaking Diao Chan, Zhao Ji, and Lady Shen. But among them, one extraordinary woman in Guangping stands apart—not just for her beauty, but for her boldness.

Mounted on a seven-meter-high bronze warhorse, a woman stands tall against the wind, her sword slicing through the air with heroic vigor, as if galloping straight out of the flames of war two thousand years ago. She is Ge E (333–280 BC), queen of King Wuling of Zhao. This trailblazing woman was the first to don *hufu* and wield a powerful bow. She even personally oversaw construction of the easternmost section of the "Southern Zhao Great Wall." Under her command, the fortress earned the name "Ge E City" and became Guangping's lasting emblem. King Wuling and Ge E—a reformist power couple—proved through action that the finest love is one forged side by side in innovation.

At dusk, the bronze horse's mane catches the golden glow of the sunset, casting a tranquil interplay of light and shadow—like memory crystallized over a thousand years. The story of this female general building fortresses and guarding the frontier is forever etched in the hearts of Guangping's people, becoming a legendary tale passed down through generations. This sculpture is not only a masterpiece of art, but also a profound tribute to a heroine who embodied courage and innovation.

磁州窑的老厂房里，古瓷片和新陶艺玩起跨界；广平水陆画里，神仙们正开着三界茶话会；固义村的傩戏面具，藏着三千年的驱邪密码。这里的每块石头都会说话，每根麦秆都能跳舞，连村民都是戏里戏外的双面人生玩家。艺术的惊喜，藏在时光的褶皱里等你来拆！

In the old factory halls of the Cizhou Kiln, ancient porcelain shards and contemporary ceramic art are crossing boundaries and sparking creativity. In the Water-and-Land Paintings of Guangping, deities gather for a cross-realm tea party. In Guyi Village, Nuo opera masks conceal three-thousand-year-old codes of exorcism and ritual. Here, every stone can speak, every stalk of wheat can dance, and even the villagers live dual lives—onstage and off. Artistic surprises lie hidden in the folds of time, waiting for you to unwrap them!

千年艺术盲盒

A Millennium-Old Artistic Surprise Box

01

来磁州窑艺术街区，看一场"陶"气变装秀
Arrive at the Cizhou Kiln Art Quarter for a "Pottery Vogue" Transformation Show

在峰峰矿区彭城镇，陶瓷七厂正经历着最浪漫的"二次烧制"。陈旧的工业骨骼里，磁州窑文化却在这里长出新的血肉——这边，古老的白地黑花在斑驳的墙下静静呼吸；那边，当代陶艺家的先锋作品在老车间里肆意绽放。

在这里，用时光烧制成的瓷片，铺就了这条通往瑰丽的小路。老厂房蜕变成文创空间，宋代梅瓶与极简咖啡杯开启时空对话，那些曾盛满古早白粥的粗陶碗，如今静静陈列，向游人细数饮食文明的变迁。来这里，最不可错过的是亲手体验环节：当夕阳为拉坯机打上柔光，捧一团彭城的陶土，沐浴在斜阳里，把独家记忆捏进磁州窑的千年传承里，送进烧炉里，在那与千年前别无二致的火焰中，熔铸成最美的岁月记号。

In Pengcheng Town, Fengfeng Mining District, the No. 7 Ceramics Factory is undergoing its most romantic "second firing." Within its time-worn industrial bones, Cizhou Kiln culture is growing new flesh. Here, ancient white-ground black-painting quietly breathes beneath mottled walls; there, avant-garde works by contemporary ceramic artists blossom freely in the old workshop.

Here, time is fired into ceramic shards that pave a path to splendor. The old factory has transformed into a cultural-creative space: a Song Dynasty Meiping vase and minimalist coffee cups begin a dialogue across time, while coarse pottery bowls, once brimming with old-style white porridge, now sit quietly on display, telling visitors the evolving story of culinary civilization. The unmissable hands-on session awaits: as the setting sun casts a soft glow on the pottery wheel, cradle a lump of Pengcheng clay in your palms, bathed in slanted sunlight, and press your unique memory into Cizhou Kiln's millennia-long heritage. Then send it into the kiln, where flames unchanged for a thousand years forge the most beautiful imprint of time.

丛台区邯郸道历史文化街区（南区）水陆画艺术展馆，水陆画文创馆 A41—1—3·No. A41-1-3, Water-and-Land Painting Art Gallery and Cultural & Creative Center, South Section, Handandao Historic and Cultural District, Congtai District

赏广平水陆画，聆听千年丹青里的跨界对话
Admire the Guangping Water-and-Land Paintings and Hear a Millennial Cross-Disciplinary Dialogue

嘘——你听，这些画里的神仙们正在开"三界茶话会"！画中，孔子与罗汉同框论道，玉帝和阎君隔卷对话。微风吹过，画中神仙似衣袂飘动，凑近些仿佛还能听见他们的窃窃私语——一场"跨界对话"正在进行。在广平诞生的水陆画，起源于三国时期的水陆法会，脱胎于礼制文化，却在文明交融的长河中，渐渐修炼出了独特的"神通"——既保留庄严仪范，又融入了生活意趣。当佛教的慈悲、道教的逍遥与儒家的礼乐在此相遇，水陆画便成了最直观的"艺术融合百科全书"。

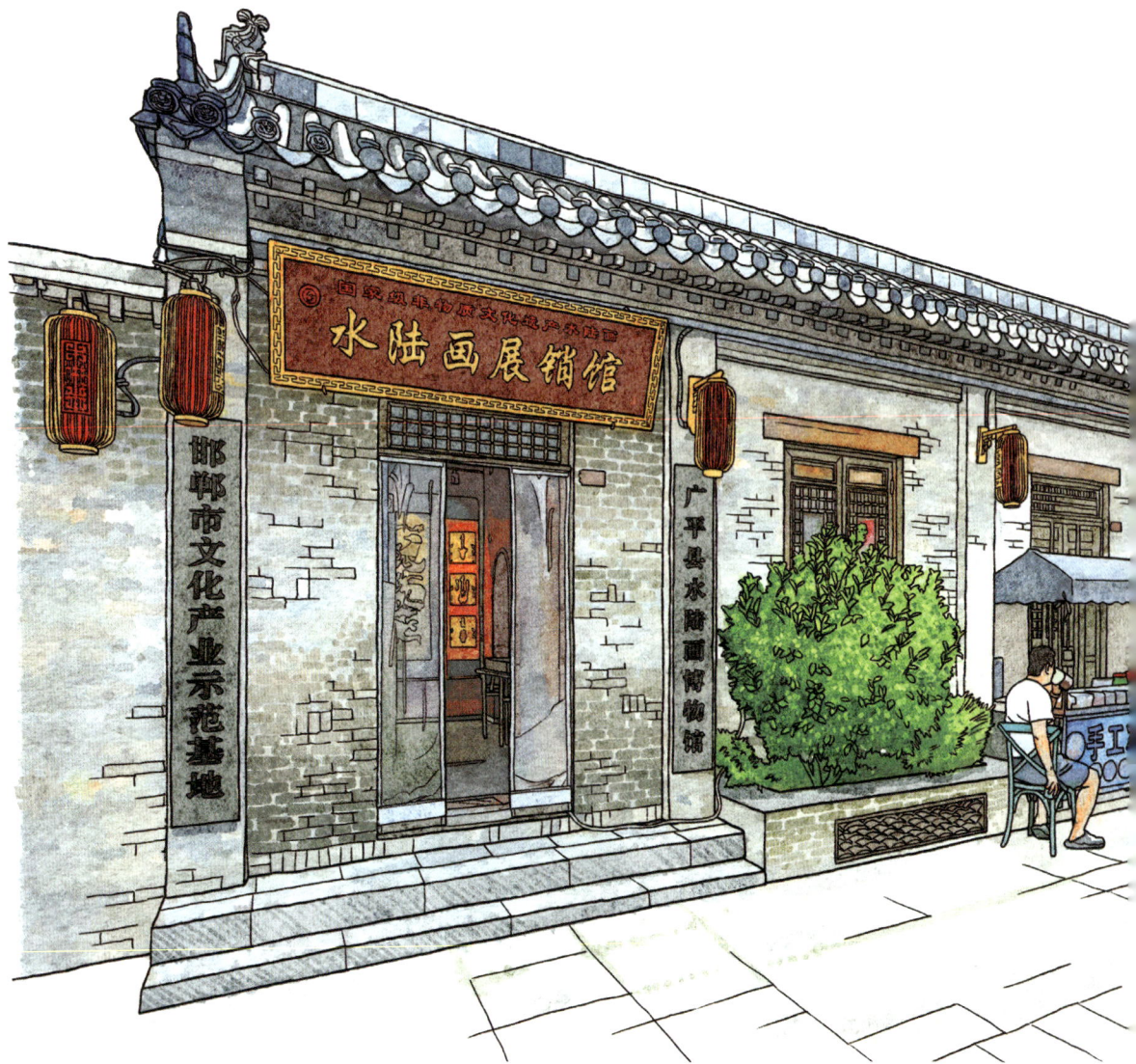

这些画卷也曾昼夜"当值"——白日受人间香火，入夜赴水陆法会。而今它们从传统仪典走向了非遗殿堂，却依然恪守着"值守"的本分：每天准时迎接八方来客，抚慰现代人的心灵，接受人们的美好祈愿。

Shh—can you hear it? The immortals in these paintings are holding a "Three Realms Tea Salon"! In the artwork, Confucius and arhats appear side by side in discussion, while the Jade Emperor and Yama converse across scrolls. When the breeze stirs, the celestial figures seem to flutter; lean in and you might even catch their whispered secrets—a "cross-disciplinary dialogue" is unfolding. The Water-and-Land Paintings born in Guangping trace their origin to the Three Kingdoms-period Water-and-Land Assemblies. Though rooted in ritual culture, they acquired a unique "divine power" through the tides of civilizational exchange—preserving solemn formality while embracing everyday charm. When Buddhist compassion, Taoist freedom, and Confucian ritual and music converge here, the Water-and-Land Paintings become the most vivid "encyclopedia of artistic fusion."

These scrolls once "stood guard" night and day—receiving earthly incense by day and attending Water-and-Land Assemblies by night. Today, they have journeyed from traditional ceremony to the halls of intangible heritage, yet still hold fast to their duty: greeting visitors from all directions each day, soothing modern souls, and receiving people's heartfelt prayers.

03

一草一世界，谱一曲指尖上的田园诗
Compose a Pastoral Poem at Your Fingertips by Blades of Grass

走进大名古城的草编非遗店铺，仿佛跌入了梦幻的绿野仙踪的世界，无处不弥漫着青草的香气，时光忽然变得柔软起来。麦秆在这里翩然起舞——非遗传承人手指翻飞，一根根金黄的草茎便乖乖地变身为憨态可掬的提包、精巧雅致的屏风，更有五彩斑斓的"草编版"脸谱跃然眼前。

当指尖触及这些草编作品，不同于工业制品的冰冷质感，这些承载着阳光记忆的天然纤维，将人掌心的温度也编织进草茎里。而今，这些麦秆盛放着大名人对土地最温柔的告白。临别不妨带只草编蚂蚱——放在你的办公桌上时刻提醒你，不要忽略生活本该有的质朴欢愉。

Step into a grass-weaving intangible-heritage shop in ancient Daming City, and it feels as if you've wandered into a dreamy world straight out of "The Wizard of Oz," filled with the scent of fresh grass—where time suddenly softens. Wheat stalks dance in the air as inheritors of the craft weave deftly—each golden blade obediently transforms into adorable tote bags, exquisitely refined screens, and even vivid "straw-woven opera masks."

When your fingertips touch these straw-woven creations, unlike the coldness of industrial goods, these natural fibers, infused with the memory of sunlight, also weave the warmth of your palm into their stems. Today, these wheat stalks bloom with the people of Daming's most tender confession to the land. Before you leave, pick up a straw-woven grasshopper. Let it rest on your desk, gently reminding you that life should be lived with simple joy.

大名草编

04

到固义村傩戏展览馆，参加一场跨越千年的"化装舞会"

Join the Thousand-Year "Masked Ball" at Guyi Village's Nuo Opera Exhibition Hall

　　商朝的巫师恐怕也没想到，三千年后，他们的"驱邪方案"会变成固义村最古老的沉浸式"化装舞会"。面具在暗处咧嘴瞪眼，或怒目圆睁，或滑稽诡谲——它们曾是村民和鬼神讨价还价的"通讯工具"，如今却成了镜头里最上镜的"表情包"。那些看似滑稽的傩舞动作，实则是古人用肢体书写的密码——有的在祈求风调雨顺，有的在演绎忠孝节义。武安傩戏的生生不息，打破了"北方无傩"的偏见。面具下的吟唱，舞步间的韵律，无不印证着华北大地同样孕育了灿烂的傩戏文化。

远处几声零星的锣响传来，商周的鬼、汉唐的妖、明清的怪，都挤在角落里交头接耳——莫慌，这只是光影和声音的戏法。这些曾经令人畏惧的面具，历经洗礼，早已化作村里的"老邻居"，在每一个节庆时分，与村民们一同守护这烟火人间。

Even Shang Dynasty shamans could hardly have imagined that three thousand years later, their "demon-exorcism rituals" would evolve into the oldest immersive "masked ball" at Guyi Village. Masks leer and glare from the shadows—some angry-eyed and round, others spooky and mischievous. Once they served as "communication tools" through which villagers negotiated with ghosts and gods; today they've become the most photogenic "emoji masks" on camera. Those seemingly comical Nuo dance moves are in fact bodily ciphers inscribed by ancient people—some prayers for good weather, some enactments of loyalty, filial piety, and virtue. The enduring vitality of Wu'an Nuo Opera breaks the stereotype that "Nuo is absent in the North." From the chanting beneath the mask to the rhythm in the footsteps, all bear witness that the vast northern plains, too, nurtured a brilliant Nuo opera culture.

From afar comes the sporadic clang of gongs—Shang-Zhou ghosts, Han-Tang demons, Ming-Qing monsters—all crowding in corners whispering to each other. Don't be alarmed—it's only a playful interplay of light and sound. Those masks, once fearsome, have endured the test of time and become the village's "old neighbors," standing with locals during every festival to protect this human world full of earthly joys.

武安市活水乡楼上村 · Loushang Village, Huoshui Township, Wu'an City

来楼上村观戏，看村民如何演绎双面人生
Watch Drama to Discover the Art of Dual Lives at Loushang Village

在武安楼上村，清晨叫醒你的不是鸡鸣，而是悠扬的练嗓声。在这里，人人都是"斜杠青年"——上午还在扛锄头下地的老把式，下午就化身平调戏中正气凛然的"黑脸包公"严正断案；方才还在灶台前煮面的村民，转眼扮成落子戏里活泼灵动的花旦舞动四方。

循着唱戏声入村，总会寻见惊艳的嗓音。忽而高亢平调穿墙而出，将古老戏文唱得荡气回肠；或遇落子戏班，竹板清脆，唱词俚俗尽显风情——这可是比脱口秀早六百年的"乡村戏剧"。

夜戏开锣时，戏台下，嗑瓜子的大娘也能随口接唱；戏台上，描眉画眼的"角儿"，明日或与你同席吃面，边捞面条边比画昨夜唱段，人人都是行走的"非遗盲盒"，就等你来"拆开"那戏里戏外的双重人生——生活即戏台，烟火亦粉墨。

In Wu'an's Loushang Village, what wakes you in the early morning isn't the cock crowing, but the melodious sound of vocal warmups. Here, everyone is a multi-hyphenate—a farmer toiling with hoes in the morning might don black-face as the upright and dignified Justice Bao in Pingdiao Opera by the afternoon; a villager cooking noodles by the stove can, in a flash, transform into the lively *huadan* (a type of young female role) of a Laozi play, dancing across the stage with spirited grace.

Follow the singing into the village, and you'll always find stunning voices. Suddenly a soaring piece of Pingdiao Opera spills through walls, filling the air with soulful echoes; or you may chance upon a Laozi troupe in rehearsal—bamboo clappers crisp, vernacular lyrics brimming with charm—this is

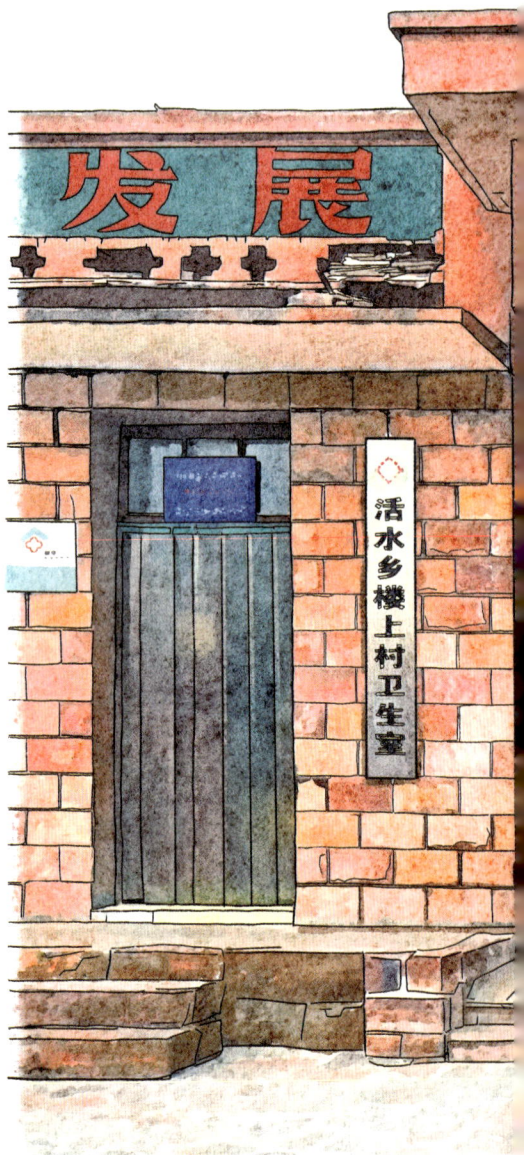

rural theatre born six centuries before modern stand-up.

When the night show begins, under stage, aunties cracking sunflower seeds in the audience will chant along casually; on stage, the painted-face "stars" might share your noodle table tomorrow, swirling noodles with one hand while miming last night's arias. Everyone here is a living "intangible heritage blind box," just waiting for you to unbox their double lives on and off stage—where daily life becomes the theater, and ordinary firelight transforms into stage makeup.

大名县天雄路与园中街交叉口东南 480 米 · 480 meters southeast of the intersection of Tianxiong Road and Yuanzhong Street, Daming County

06

石上书，灯下阁，来大名听一首博物馆夜曲
Come Daming Stone Carving Museum to Hear a Nocturne

　　大名县藏着一座"会说话"的石头图书馆——大名石刻博物馆。这里的每一块石碑都是穿越千年的"老学究"，有的"穿唐装"，有的"戴宋冠"，正用斑驳的刻痕向你讲述岁月的变迁。五礼记碑以"唐碑宋承"的奇观巍然矗立，成就"碑刻之最"的美誉；何弘敬墓志铭以"天下第一"之姿青睐时光，近两米高的青石篆刻三代节度使风云。马文操神道碑以飘逸行书打破陈规，开创行书入碑新风。

　　夜幕降临，月色与灯火在弘敬阁上相撞，整座博物馆倏然化作露天历史剧场，上演着跨越古今的光影传奇。临走之前，别忘了体验一回拓片制作——让宣纸与石刻亲密相拥，将春秋笔墨拓印成独属于你的完美"石"光。

In Daming County lies a "talking" stone library—the Daming Stone Carving Museum. Each stele here is a millennium-travelling "old scholar," some dressed in Tang garb, others wearing Song dynasty caps, all speaking to you through weathered inscriptions about the passage of time. The Stele of the Five Rites stands tall as a marvel of "Tang stele, Song continuation," earning praise as the pinnacle of inscribed monuments; the Epitaph of He Hongjing commands time's favor as the "number one under heaven," its nearly two-meter green stone etched with the legacies of three generations of military governors. The Spirit-Way Stele of Ma Wencao, with its flowing cursive, broke conventions and pioneered the use of running script in stone.

At dusk, when moonlight and lantern light collide at the Hongjing Pavilion, the entire museum transforms into an open-air historical theater, staging a light-and-shadow legend that bridges past and present. Before you leave, don't forget to try your hand at rubbing—let Xuan paper embrace the stone and imprint ancient brushstrokes into your very own perfect "stone light."

永年区永合会镇吴庄村北 · North of Wuzhuang Village,
Yonghehui Town, Yongnian District

来朱山石刻，破译字里行间的摩崖密语
Decode the Cliffside Secret Messages in Zhushan Stone Inscriptions

登上朱山之巅，那方摩崖石刻赫然映入眼帘："赵廿二年八月丙寅群臣上醻此石北"。斑驳的十五个字，涵盖了群臣为君王祈福的盛况。凝神静听，字里行间似有觥筹交错的回响，和着山风送来"王上万年"的低声祝祷。更有趣的是三朝石刻的时空布局——西汉与东汉石刻相隔二十一米，恰似两汉更替的留白；而唐代石刻又向东十五米，仿佛要为盛唐再拓一方天地。从字体的变化得以窥见朝代的更迭，从刻痕的消腐得以见证岁月的沧桑。若细观之，或可发现某个字迹略显歪斜——那定是凿刻时，被山间突然飞过的燕雀分了神。

　　夕阳西下，山风翻动游人的衣袂，仿佛邀人共赴一场千年雅集。这时不妨效仿石刻行礼之姿，打卡留念，将这鎏金暮色与朱山石刻的相遇瞬间，永恒定格。

Atop Zhushan Mountain, you'll find a cliffside inscription reading, "In the 22nd year of Zhao, eighth lunar month, *bingyin* day (a celestial stem-branch date), ministers presented wine north of this rock." Those fifteen weathered characters capture the grand ceremony of ministers offering blessings for their king. Focus, and between the lines you can almost hear clinking cups and the mountain breeze carrying whispered blessings of "ten thousand years to the king." Even more intriguing is the spatial layering of inscriptions from three dynasties—the Western and Eastern Han carvings sit 21 meters apart, echoing the Han transition's gap; the Tang-era inscription lies 15 meters further east, as if carving out a fresh realm for the flourishing Tang. The changing calligraphy reveals dynastic shifts; the weathered grooves testify to time's erosion. Look closely and you might spot a slightly skewed character—surely the carver was distracted by a sparrow flitting by.

As the sun sets, and the mountain wind billows through your cloak, it's as if you're invited to a refined gathering spanning a thousand years. Try mimicking the carved saluting posture for your photo—immortalizing your moment with Zhushan's stone inscriptions in gilded twilight.

馆陶县寿山寺乡寿山寺东村内 · In Shoushansidong Village, Shoushansi Township, Guantao County

来馆陶粮画小镇，围观五谷"变形记"
Witness the Metamorphosis of Cereals in Guantao Grain Painting Town

当五谷杂粮遇上匠人指尖，麦粒、红豆、绿豆便成了颜料——这里是馆陶粮画小镇，一个让粮食"不务正业"的艺术江湖。在这里，五谷杂粮，不仅能填饱肚子，更能演绎艺术，演绎时光——看那幅轰动国际的粮画《清明上河图》，用七万颗精心挑选的谷物在画板上"复活"了汴京盛景。藏家一掷万金，买走的何止是艺术品，分明是一卷"可食用"的北宋市井画卷。

游览之时，不妨到工坊小试身手，用镊子当画笔，拿五谷作颜料，体验"种"一幅画的乐趣，把"粒粒皆辛苦"变成"粒粒皆艺术"。粮画小镇，等你发现：人间至味，不止于舌尖，更在这方寸画板之上——我们可以用五谷作颜料，以大地为画纸，绘出自己的画卷。

When grains meet artisans' fingertips, wheat, red beans, and mung beans become pigments—welcome to Guantao Grain Painting Town, an artistic realm where grain goes "off-duty." Here, grains not only fill bellies—they evoke and depict the passage of time. Behold the internationally acclaimed grain painting *Along the River During the Qingming Festival*, where 70,000 meticulously selected kernels revive the bustling scene of Bianjing. When a collector paid a fortune, they bought more than art—they acquired an edible scroll of Northern Song urban life.

During your visit, stop by the workshop to try your hand—tweezers as brush, grains as pigment—experiencing the joy of "sowing" a painting. Turn "all grains are hard work" into "every grain is art." Grain Painting Town awaits your discovery: that the greatest flavors of life lie not only on the tongue, but upon this tiny canvas—with grains as our pigments and soil as our parchment, we paint the masterpiece of existence.

当娲皇宫的青铜风铃在太行山巅响起，当响堂山的第一缕晨光穿透北魏佛龛，邯郸的三千年文明便在砖瓦纹样间苏醒。邯郸的厚重，不在史册的墨迹里，而在每一块执拗守望的砖石中。

When the bronze wind chimes of the Nüwa Palace ring out atop the Taihang Mountains, when the first ray of dawn pierces the Northern Wei Dynasty Buddhist niches at Xiangtang Mountain, Handan's three thousand years of civilization awaken in the patterns of brick and tile. Handan's weightiness is not found in the inked pages of history books, but in each stubborn brick and stone that stands sentinel through the ages.

赵都古建拼图

The Architectural Puzzle of the Zhao Capital

01

绝顶娲皇宫，蓬莱欲比仙
Ascend to Nüwa Palace, a Fairyland Rivaling Penglai

在太行绝壁间，娲皇宫凌空而立，这里相传为女娲抟土造人、炼石补天之地。山上、山下两部分建筑以十八盘山道相连，曲折婀娜，陡然巍峨。每逢农历三月，当地人会共祭女娲诞辰，"华夏祖庙"香火由此而千年不绝。

其中，娲皇阁最令人称奇——八根铁索如流星垂落，将楼阁系于绝壁之上，每当楼体前倾，铁索绷直回拽，造就"风过微颤，危而不坠，屹立千年"的奇观，"活楼吊庙"的称呼由此得名。崖壁上，北齐摩崖刻经饱经沧桑仍清晰可辨，这部"天下第一壁经"见证了女娲信仰与佛教文化的交融。

若问娲皇宫最动人处何在？或许正是这种奇绝建筑与神话信仰的交融结合——就像那八根铁索，上系危楼，下连地脉；既牵着飘摇的楼阁，也系着中华文明生生不息的根脉。

Perched precariously on the sheer cliffs of the Taihang Mountains, Nüwa Palace is said to be the very site where the goddess Nüwa molded humans from clay and mended the sky with stones. The complex consists of two parts—one on the mountain and one below—linked by a winding mountain path of eighteen switchbacks, both graceful and steep. Each year in the third lunar month, locals gather to celebrate Nüwa's birthday, and the incense of this "Ancestral Temple of Huaxia" has burned for a thousand years.

Most astonishing is the Nüwa Pavilion: eight iron chains cascade down like meteors, securing the structure to the cliff face. As the building leans forward, the chains pull taut, creating a spectacle known as "trembling in the wind, precarious yet unfallen, standing firm for a thousand years." Thus, it has earned the name "living tower-hung temple."

On the cliff wall beside it, Northern Qi scripture carvings remain clearly legible despite the ravages of time—this "first scripture wall under heaven" bears witness to the fusion of Nüwa worship and Buddhist culture.

What is the most captivating aspect of Nüwa Palace? Perhaps it lies in the union of myth and architecture—like those eight iron chains: tethered above to the swaying pavilion, anchored below to the pulse of the earth, they bind not just the structure to the rock, but also the roots of Chinese civilization across time.

打卡皇家石窟，来一场跨越时空的凝视
Gaze Across Time at the Imperial Grottoes

邯郸西南部，一片青葱地貌间，藏着一座皇家石窟——响堂山石窟。这座石窟分南北两处，相距十五公里，有洞窟三十七座，大小雕像四千四百二十二尊，刻经十三部。因为石窟内构造奇特，人们击掌、甩袖等动作都能发出洪亮的回声，所以称为"响堂山"。

响堂山石窟始建于东魏，与云冈、龙门并称中国三大皇家石窟，其上承北魏余续、下开唐风先河的独特风格被称为"北齐样式"。其中，大佛洞是响堂山石窟中规模最大、开凿最早的，其佛像眉眼微闭，姿态和谐，引得古今无数信众前来参拜。傍晚，晚霞给佛像镶了层金边，那一刻，千年的文明好像眨了下眼，仿佛在说："嘿，我可等到你啦。"

Amidst the verdant landscapes of southwestern Handan lies an imperial cave temple—the Xiangtangshan Grotto Complex. Divided into North and South sections, 15 kilometers apart, the site today preserves 37 caves, more than 4,422 statues, and 13 scripture carvings. Due to the caves' unusual acoustics—where a clap or swish of a sleeve produces powerful echoes—the site is called "Xiangtangshan," or Echo Hall Mountain.

The Xiangtangshan Grotto Complex was first carved during the Eastern Wei Dynasty and, together with Yungang and Longmen, is considered one of the Three Great Imperial Grottoes of China. Its unique fusion style, bridging the remnants of Northern Wei (386–534) and the emerging Tang aesthetics, became known as the "Northern Qi style." The Great Buddha Cave is the largest and earliest of the grottoes here—its Buddha statue, eyes gently closed and posture serene, has drawn countless worshippers throughout history. At dusk, when the evening glow gilds the statue's edges with light, it feels as if a thousand years of civilization has blinked—whispering, "Hey, I've been waiting for you."

03

到常乐寺，拍一张《华夏地理》同款照片
Capture a Photo Worthy of *National Geographic China* at Changle Temple

被唐代文人称为"河朔第一古刹"的常乐寺，不仅是普通的佛教圣地，还是一位传奇皇帝的落幕舞台。步入常乐寺，仿佛一脚踏进了东魏北齐的时光褶皱——这里曾是北齐神武皇帝高欢的陵寝，见证了这位北齐霸主的人生句点。

常乐寺遗址的无头佛像，和着周围荒凉的山林，以残缺之姿，反倒成就了另一种圆满——斑驳的庙宇内，北齐的痕迹犹在；无头佛像上，是与古人共同凝望过的蓝天月夜。当夕阳掠过散落的石柱旧碑，投下参差的光影，整座遗址便成了胶片暗房，仿佛历史的轮廓正在显影，洗印出千年之前的旧照。那些不经意间邂逅的绝美光影，宛如《华夏地理》封面的神来之笔，都是常乐寺对有缘人的馈赠。

Lauded by Tang Dynasty literati as "the foremost ancient temple north of the Yellow River," Changle Temple is more than a sacred Buddhist site—it is also the final chapter in the life of a legendary emperor. Walking into Changle Temple is like stepping into the time-worn folds of the Eastern Wei and Northern Qi dynasties. Once the resting place of Gao Huan (496–547), Emperor Shenwu of Northern Qi, the site bears silent witness to the conclusion of a powerful reign.

Headless Buddha statues stand amid desolate hills, and in their brokenness lies a unique form of completeness. Within the weathered temple walls, traces of Northern Qi craftsmanship endure; above the neckless figures, the same sky and moonlight once shared with the ancients still shine. When the setting sun spills across the scattered stone pillars and worn steles, the entire site becomes a darkroom of memory—developing outlines of history like vintage film, printing images from a thousand years ago. The stunning light and shadow you stumble upon here, accidental yet divine, could rival the covers of *National Geographic China*. They are Changle Temple's gift to those destined hearts.

04

峰峰矿区太行东路 · Taihang East Road, Fengfeng Mining District

登玉皇阁，破解四百年前的力学魔术

Climb the Yuhuang Pavilion and Unravel a Ming Dynasty Engineering Secret

在太行八陉之一——滏口陉的古道上，一座明代建筑格外引人注目——这就是堪称"建筑界伪装大师"的纸坊玉皇阁。这座建筑仿佛跟来往行人开了四百年的"玩笑"——它明明浑身是砖，却偏要把自己"打扮"成木结构建筑的模样！不用一木一梁，仅凭青砖叠涩，便凌空而起，成就了现存明代无梁殿建筑的典范。拾级而入，抬眼望去，明代琉璃屋顶宝刹巍然，三颗宝珠熠熠生辉；屋脊之上藻纹如波，人物栩栩，仿佛游龙穿行于花树之间，处处彰显着匠人的鬼斧神工。

登临玉皇阁，抚触被晒暖的砖石，仿佛还能感受到数百年前的匠心余温。玉皇阁早已证明：不止金碧辉煌才可以被历史铭记，青砖黑瓦亦能书写光阴的诗篇。

Along the ancient path of Fukou Pass, one of the Eight Passes of the Taihang Mountains, stands a striking Ming Dynasty structure—Zhifang Yuhuang Pavilion, often hailed as the "master of architectural disguise." Rising high above, this building has played a 400-year-old trick on passersby: though made entirely of brick, it insists on appearing as a wooden structure! Without a single beam or plank, it ascends through staggered brickwork alone, standing as a model among existing beamless halls of the Ming Dynasty. Climbing the steps within, one looks up to see the Ming-style glazed-tile roof with its gleaming spires—three jewel-like ornaments sparkle overhead. Along the ridgeline, wave-like patterns and vivid figures dance among flowering trees, showcasing the artisans' exquisite craftsmanship.

At the summit, place your hand on the sun-warmed bricks. You may still feel the lingering warmth of centuries-old devotion. Yuhuang Pavilion long ago proved: history need not be recorded only in gold and jade; even humble bricks and tiles can compose a timeless verse.

05

一锅黄粱未熟，一梦千年未醒
One Pot Uncooked, One Dream Unwoken for a Thousand Years

　　步入黄粱梦吕仙祠，便能理解那个流传了一千多年的美梦为何在此生根。沿中轴线自南向北，钟离殿内的钟离权像神态威严，吕祖殿里吕洞宾仙风道骨，卢生殿中那尊卢生侧卧像嘴角微扬，仿佛仍在未醒的美梦之中。

　　吕仙祠始建于唐末宋初，传说吕洞宾曾在此点化卢生。卢生在梦里尝尽一生：少年得志登进士，官至宰相位尊荣，五世同堂天伦乐，八十寿终享正寝，醒后一切皆幻灭，不过黄粱饭未熟。吕祖殿的香火缠绕着房梁，那慈眉善目的吕洞宾正捻须含笑，看那展

列的青瓷枕，仿佛仍凝聚着当年灶火的余温。不过怀揣好梦的不再是卢生，而是如今过往的游人。

或许，漫步在黄粱梦吕仙祠，你也能听见吕仙悠语："功名富贵皆幻境，不如枕上悟浮生。"

Step into the Lüzu Temple of the Yellow Millet Dream, and you'll understand why a beautiful dream that has endured for over a millennium took root here. Moving north along the central axis, you'll encounter the solemn figure of Zhongli Quan in the Zhongli Hall, the immortal grace of Lü Dongbin in the Lüzu Hall, and in the Lu Sheng Hall, a reclining statue of Lu Sheng with a faint smile—as if still lost in a dream that has yet to end.

The temple was first built during the late Tang and early Song dynasties, and legend holds that Lü Dongbin once enlightened Lu Sheng here. In his dream, Lu Sheng lived an entire life: rising as a young scholar, ascending to the esteemed rank of prime minister, enjoying the joys of five generations under one roof, and dying peacefully at the age of eighty—only to awaken and find it had all vanished. Nothing was left but the millet porridge, still simmering unfinished. Fragrant incense curls around the beams of the Lüzu Hall, and Lü Dongbin, with a kind smile and gently stroked beard, seems to watch over the glazed ceramic pillow on display, as if it still holds the warmth of that ancient stove fire. But the one carrying the dream is no longer Lu Sheng—it is now the passing visitor of today.

Perhaps, as you stroll through the Lüzu Temple of the Yellow Millet Dream, you, too, might hear Lü Dongbin's soft immortal whisper: "Fame and fortune are illusions. Better to awaken on your pillow to the fleeting nature of life."

06

来武安，与舍利塔共沐千载斜阳
Bathe in the Sunset with the Relic Pagoda in Wu'an

"梵音已杳招提远，唯有钟声恋故人"。数百年前的这句咏叹，至今仍在塔檐间低徊。这座建于宋景祐三年的密檐式砖塔，是邯郸地区现存最完整的宋塔，十三层塔檐渐次收分，如展开的经卷；八角棱柱挺拔而立，似凝固的梵音。千年过去，塔檐风铃依旧轻吟着"燕舞浮屠十三层"的绝唱。

如今古塔已深深融入武安人的文化血脉，成为城市的精神地标。晨光中，古塔仿佛一支立在武安天际线上的毛笔，写下千年的信仰；夜幕下，精心设计的景观照明让古塔焕发新生，市民们在此散步纳凉，塔前广场变身孩子们的乐园与课堂；每逢春节，在塔前拍摄全家福已成为传统，那些珍藏在手机里的塔影，化作游子最深刻的乡愁。

"The chanting fades, the temple distant—only the bell lingers, longing for old friends." This centuries-old verse still echoes softly beneath the eaves of the pagoda. Built in the third year of Jingyou era (1036) during the Song Dynasty, this brick pagoda with multiple eaves is the most well-preserved Song pagoda in the Handan region. Its thirteen stories recede gradually like an unfolding sutra scroll; its octagonal column stands tall like a frozen chant. A thousand years later, the wind chimes beneath its eaves still softly sing the refrain: "Swallows circle the thirteen levels of the stupa."

Today, the ancient pagoda is deeply woven into the cultural fabric of Wu'an, a spiritual landmark for the city. In the morning light, the tower resembles a calligraphy brush standing against the Wu'an skyline, dipping into the shimmering Minghe River to inscribe a thousand years of faith. By nightfall, carefully designed lighting breathes new life into the structure. Locals stroll and cool off here, and the square in front becomes both a playground and classroom for children. Each Spring Festival, taking a family portrait before the tower has become a cherished tradition. Those tower images saved on phones have become a tangible memory—a profound expression of homesickness for those far from home.

07

在二祖匡教寺，遇见千年前的佛系生活
Find Zen Life from a Thousand Years Ago at Erzu Kuangjiao Temple

在晨雾中，一座始建于唐代的古寺，正轻轻抖落历史的尘埃。二祖匡教寺被视为中国禅宗发源地，得到达摩大师真传的佛教禅宗二祖慧可大师曾在这里讲经说法，延续达摩大师的禅宗法脉。而在不远处的元符寺，安奉着禅宗二祖慧可大师的真身舍利，珍藏着见证中国禅宗发展的活化石——达摩大师碑。这座与少林寺达摩碑、空相寺达摩碑齐名的三大达摩碑之一，历经千年沉睡后重见天日。

二祖匡教寺，历经兴废，历代都有重建，每一道砖缝里都藏着光阴的记号，每一片新漆下都覆盖着古老的故事。不妨在暮鼓响起时，坐在那株慧可手植柏的树影里，看夕阳一字一句地为碑文描金，仿佛是一位小沙弥在默读，又好像一位高僧在专心雕琢，带着我们感悟生活的智慧。

In the morning mist, a temple first built during the Tang Dynasty gently shakes off the dust of time. The Erzu Kuangjiao Temple is revered as the cradle of Chinese Zen Buddhism, where Master Huike (487–593)—the Second Patriarch who inherited Bodhidharma's authentic transmission— expounded the Dharma and perpetuated the Zen lineage. Nearby, the Yuanfu Temple enshrines the true relics of Master Huike and preserves a living fossil of Chinese Zen heritage—the Stele of Bodhidharma. Ranked alongside the Bodhidharma steles of Shaolin Temple and Kongxiang Temple, it is one of the three great steles of its kind, now reemerging after a millennium of slumber.

The Erzu Kuangjiao Temple has seen cycles of decline and renewal. Every crack in its bricks holds the imprints of time; every new coat of paint conceals ancient tales. When the evening bell tolls, sit beneath the shadow of the cypress planted by Huike himself, and watch as the setting sun traces golden lines across the stele's inscription—like a novice monk silently reciting a verse, or a master diligently carving wisdom into stone. In this quiet light, we begin to grasp life's deeper truths.

08

到南响堂，听一场千年之前的"音乐会"
Hear a Concert from a Thousand Years Ago at South Xiangtangshan Grottoes

滏阳河的晨光轻轻覆满山崖，南响堂石窟如初醒的交响乐团，正要奏响千年梵音。其中最为嘹亮的千佛洞，正以覆钵塔形之姿凌于滏水之畔。

走进千佛洞，迎面便能看到那斗拱窟檐以上凿大形覆钵，钵中央雕刻展翅欲飞的金翅鸟，好似正在发出响亮的鸣叫。往里深入，走进窟中，映入眼帘的是它前壁满雕塑千佛，其他三壁又凿一大龛，内均一佛二弟子两菩萨。壁上部也各雕千佛，下设基坛，窟顶微隆，雕莲花和八尊伎乐天，形象生动、美观，一众佛塑嘴唇微启，似在讲经，那穿越千年的梵音仿佛不绝于耳。

Morning light from the Fuyang River gently drapes the cliffs, and the South Xiangtangshan Grottoes stir like an awakening symphony, ready to perform a thousand-year-old chant. The most resounding among them is the Thousand Buddha Cave, rising by the Fuyang River in the shape of an inverted-bowl stupa.

Enter the Thousand Buddha Cave, and you are greeted by a large, inverted bowl-shaped dome carved above the eaved brackets. At its center is a Garuda with wings outstretched, poised as if to cry out in flight. Deeper inside, the front wall is densely carved with a thousand Buddhas, while each of the other three walls contains a large niche housing one Buddha, two disciples, and two bodhisattvas. The upper sections of the walls are also adorned with a thousand Buddhas, and the base features a foundation platform. The slightly domed ceiling is decorated with a lotus blossom and eight celestial musicians—vivid, graceful, and expressive. The lips of the Buddha figures are slightly parted, as if still delivering sermons. Across the span of time, the chant of dharma seems to echo unceasingly.

09

永年区广府古城城东 25 公里的东桥村 · Dongqiao Village, 25 kilometers east of Guangfu Ancient City, Yongnian District

在弘济桥，见证滏阳河"摆渡人"的坚守
Witness the Devotion of the "Ferry Keeper" of the Fuyang River at Hongji Bridge

"几番留恋古城东，皆此桥飞滏水中。"据万历年间记载，这座与赵州桥齐名的"姊妹桥"——弘济桥早已在此"执勤"了无数春秋。其以天然石料作为主要建筑材料，形式美观，结构坚固，桥面斑驳坎坷，深浅印记间，犹闻商旅驼铃，似见农家车辙。桥两侧有横三纵四的寸许深槽，最有可能是当地纤夫经年累月留下的纤痕。桥栏上的石狮经岁月摩挲，温润如玉。细观栏板内侧，可见猛虎、灵鹿、祥瑞麒麟等浮雕，更有寓意深远的民间故事点缀其间，寄托了两岸人共同的美好祝愿。而最令人叹服的，当数拱顶两侧的吸水兽，数百年来，吸水兽威镇滏阳河，守护一方安宁，使洪水鲜少肆虐。

暮色中的石桥，倒映在波光里，叠印着古今行人的身影，如一部岁月"石"书——不拒绝变迁，亦不失本真，在流转的时光里，让每一段故事都经桥而过，留下脚印。

"So many times I've lingered on the city's east—always drawn to this bridge spanning the Fuyang River." According to records from its reconstruction during the Wanli reign (1573–1620) of the Ming Dynasty, the "sister bridge" to the famed Zhaozhou Bridge—Hongji Bridge—has long stood its post through countless seasons. Constructed using natural stone, the bridge is both visually elegant and structurally robust. The surface bears uneven weathering, its deep and shallow impressions echoing with the sounds of merchant caravans and the ruts of rural carts. On both sides of the bridge deck are grid-like grooves, three horizontal and four vertical, each about an inch deep, likely the wear marks left by years of labor

from local towpath workers. The lion-topped stone balustrades, polished by centuries of touch, gleam with a warm luster. Look closely at the inner panels of the railings, and you'll see bas-reliefs of fierce tigers, spiritual deer, and auspicious *qilin* (Chinese unicorn), alongside folk stories rich in symbolism and heartfelt wishes from those on both banks. Most awe-inspiring are the water-draining beasts at the base of each arch. For centuries, they've stood guard over the Fuyang River, protecting the region from floods.

In twilight, the stone bridge reflects on the shimmering surface of the river, overlapping images of ancient and modern travelers alike. It becomes a stone scroll of time—embracing change without losing its essence, allowing every passing story to leave its mark upon its path.

　　从赤岸村的烽火指挥到响堂铺的伏击硝烟，从晋冀鲁豫边区的政权探索到地下长城的军民智慧，邯郸处处藏着热血沸腾的红色故事，处处镌刻着革命先辈的热血与担当，凝成了永不褪色的精神坐标。

　　From the signal command fires of Chi'an Village to the ambush smoke of Xiangtangpu, from the political experiments of the Shanxi-Hebei-Shandong-Henan Border Region to the military-civil ingenuity of the Underground Great Wall, every corner of Handan hides stories of red-hot revolutionary fervor. Etched into its landscape are the courage and commitment of those who came before, a spiritual compass that never fades.

第五章
Chapter 5

红色能量
补给站

A Red Spirit Revival Station

01

到赤岸村，解锁太行的热血副本
Charge into Chi'an Village and Open the Chapter of Heroic Taihang Adventures

  这不是游戏剧情，而是一段真实的高燃历史。1940年，刘伯承、邓小平率领八路军一二九师进驻涉县赤岸村，在这个太行山深处的"战时指挥中心"，创造了"小米加步枪"的红色传奇——煤油灯下，他们用铅笔在地图上画出三万多次战斗的轨迹。史料记载，抗日战争和解放战争时期，革命的星火在太行山燎原，这里走出了两位元帅和三百六十四位将军。如今，在赤岸村旁的将军岭上，安息着刘伯承元帅等共和国将帅，这里的每一株草木都在诉说那段金戈铁马的峥嵘岁月。这座用鲜血浇灌的山岭，已成为永恒的精神坐标，见证着从战火纷飞到和平发展的伟大征程。

  这里不是历史课堂，而是跨次元的时空对话。当你在首长们亲手栽种的紫荆树下捡起一片落叶，太行山的风会悄悄告诉你，这里的每一块石头，都是革命先辈改写中国命运的见证者。如今，这座拥有九百年历史的古村落，已成为中国美丽乡村建设的典范之一。当革命红与生态绿融合，历史的脉动依然在满山葱郁中生生不息。

  This isn't a game storyline—it's a chapter of history ablaze with passion. In 1940, Liu Bocheng (1892–1986) and Deng Xiaoping (1904–1997) led the Eighth Route Army's 129th Division into Chi'an Village in Shexian County, transforming this deep Taihang mountain village into a "wartime command center" and creating the red legend of "millet plus rifle." Beneath the glow of kerosene lamps, they sketched the paths of over 30,000 military operations with pencil on paper maps. According to historical records, during the War of Resistance Against Japanese Aggression and the War of Liberation, the revolutionary spark blazed across the Taihang Mountains.

From here emerged 2 marshals and 364 generals. Today, on General's Ridge beside Chi'an Village, Marshal Liu Bocheng and other military leaders of the People's Republic of China rest in peace. Every blade of grass and leaf on this blood-soaked mountain bears witness to those tumultuous and valiant years. This ridge, nourished by sacrifice, has become a permanent spiritual landmark, and a testament to the journey from wartime turmoil to peaceful development.

This is not a history class, but a cross-dimensional dialogue through time. When you pick up a fallen leaf beneath the Chinese redbud trees planted by the commanders themselves, the wind of the Taihang will gently tell you: every stone here bears witness to how revolutionary forebears reshaped China's destiny. Today, this ancient village with a 900-year history has become a model of China's Beautiful Countryside initiative. As the red of revolution merges with the green of ecology, the pulse of history continues to beat strong in these verdant hills.

02

在晋冀鲁豫烈士陵园，瞻仰热血浇筑的永恒丰碑

Pay Tribute to an Eternal Monument Forged in Blood at the Jinjiluyu Martyrs Cemetery

　　邯郸的心脏地带，坐落着新中国成立后的第一座大型烈士陵园——晋冀鲁豫烈士陵园。该陵园于1946年奠基，1950年落成，两百多名为国捐躯的英烈长眠于此。

　　拾级而上，烈士纪念塔巍然耸立，直指苍穹。毛主席题写的"英勇牺牲的烈士们千古无上光荣"鎏金大字，在阳光的映照下熠熠生辉。左权将军墓前，白菊常新——这位抗日战争中牺牲的八路军最高级别将领，用生命铸就了太行山般永恒的脊梁。陵园内，座座墓碑整齐肃立，每一座都铭刻着一段炽热燃烧的青春。微风过处，如诉当年烽火；玉兰花开，宛若家书未寄。今山河无恙，愿英魂永安！这永不褪色的精神坐标，正将红色革命的记忆凝成永恒。

　　In the heart of Handan lies the first large-scale martyrs cemetery established after the founding of the People's Republic of China, the Jinjiluyu Martyrs Cemetery. Laid out in 1946 and completed in 1950, it is the final resting place of over 200 heroic martyrs who sacrificed their lives for the nation.

　　Climbing the steps, the Martyrs' Memorial Tower rises solemnly, piercing the heavens. Chairman Mao Zedong's gilded inscription, "The martyrs who died heroically are eternally glorious," glows brightly in the sun. Before the tomb of General Zuo Quan (1905–1942), highest-ranking Eighth Route Army officer to fall in the War of Resistance Against Japanese Aggression, fresh white chrysanthemums are ever renewed. With his life, he cast an eternal backbone as unshakable as the Taihang Mountains. Within the cemetery, the orderly rows of tombstones stand in solemn reverence, each etched with a tale of youth ignited in flame. Where the breeze whispers, echoes of wartime cannon fire still seem to stir; when the magnolias bloom, they carry the weight of unsent letters home. Today, the mountains and rivers stand secure. May the heroic souls rest forever in peace. This unfading spiritual landmark crystallizes the memory of the red revolution into eternity.

03

到弹音村，探访新中国政权建设的"试验田"
Travel to Tanyin Village, Exploring the "Experimental Field" of New China's Governance

　　走进涉县弹音村的晋冀鲁豫边区政府旧址，时间仿佛在这里凝固。1942 至 1945 年，晋冀鲁豫边区政府在此驻扎三年，为新中国的政权建设描绘出了最初的蓝图。

　　推开门，时光在此沉淀。边区政府办公厅、高等法院等旧址错落排列。陈列室内，泛黄的布告上字迹依然清晰，那些手写的政令仿佛还留存着起草时的余温。这里开创性地建立了相对完整的政权体系，从"三三制"民主选举到精兵简政，从发展经济到改善民生，每一项探索都为新中国积累了宝贵经验。临别回望，突然明白：伟大的事业，往往始于最朴实的坚持。

　　Entering Tanyin Village in Shexian County, once the site of the former Shanxi-Hebei-Shandong-Henan Border Region Government, one feels as though time has frozen within these walls. From 1942 to 1944, the border-region government remained in residence for three years, laying the initial blueprint of China's future governance.

　　Pushing open the door, it seems as if time has settled here. The offices of the Border Region Government, the High Court, and other aged facilities remain arrayed in balance. In the exhibition hall, yellowed bulletins with neat handwriting still remain legible, as though their creators' warmth lingers. This site was the birthplace of a relatively complete governance system. From the "three-thirds system" democratic elections to streamlining the government, from economic development to improving people's livelihoods, each experiment provided valuable lessons for the New China. As you depart, glancing back, you realize: great undertakings often begin with the simplest perseverance.

晋冀鲁豫边区政府旧址

04

涉县 309 国道与 225 乡道交叉口东南约 220 米 · About 220 meters southeast of the intersection of National Highway 309 and Township Road 225, Shexian County

寻踪响堂铺，在弹痕松涛间触碰热血的温度
Seek Xiangtangpu to Touch the Heat of Valor Amid the Scars and Pines

巍巍太行山，镌刻着一部永不褪色的红色史诗。1937 年，八路军东渡黄河，在这片热土上谱写了气壮山河的抗战篇章。

走进响堂铺伏击战遗址，山崖间仿佛仍回荡着 1938 年的枪炮声——徐向前指挥的这场经典伏击战，一举歼灭日寇四百余人。抚摸残留的弹痕，依稀能感受到当年战士们无畏牺牲的勇气和革命的血性。这里不需要宏大叙事，当你触摸发烫的山石，聆听松涛里裹挟着的冲锋号声，突然就懂了，真正的沉浸式体验，是感受那一段段仍在山河脉搏里跳动的青春；突然就明白，英雄从未离去，他们早已化作这方水土的脊梁。

In the majestic folds of the Taihang Mountains is etched a red epic that will never fade. In 1937 the Eighth Route Army crossed the Yellow River and composed a stirring chapter of the War of Resistance Against Japanese Aggression on this land steeped in revolutionary fervor.

At the site of the Xiangtangpu ambush, echoes of the gunfire from 1938 still seem to reverberate among the cliffs. In this classic ambush operation directed by Xu Xiangqian (1901–1990), one of the founding marshals of New China, successfully eliminated more than 400 Japanese troops. As your hand traces the bullet holes still left on the rock face, you can almost sense the soldiers' fearless sacrifice and revolutionary resolve. There is no need for grand narratives here. When you place your palm on the sun-warmed mountain stone and listen to the wind in the pines carrying the distant sound of a bugle charge, it suddenly clicks: the truest immersive experience is feeling the heartbeat of youthful sacrifice that still pulses through the land. And in that moment, you will understand: heroes never truly leave since they have long become the backbone of this land.

05

寻访新华社旧址，在铅字与电波中触摸新闻的脉搏
Trace the Former Site of Xinhua News Agency to Feel the Pulse of Journalism in Movable Type and Radio Waves

"纤笔一枝谁与似？三千毛瑟精兵。"毛泽东这首《临江仙》中的词句，得到了最生动的诠释。1946年夏，晋冀鲁豫人民日报社与新华社晋冀鲁豫总分社在此合署办公。这里的每一支笔，都化作了直指敌人心脏的钢枪利炮。

进入院落，时光仿佛倒回到那个烽火连天的年代，麻油灯下伏案的编辑，庙宇里拣字的工人，守护印刷窑洞的民兵……在这里，他们创造了红色新闻的奇迹，让晋冀鲁豫《人民日报》从这里发出时代强音。还有那些传承的故事：王春、张磐石等新闻前辈，在战火中言传身教，培养出新中国第一批红色新闻工作者。如今，阳光斜照的窗棂间，依稀可闻铅字落版的清响，可见那些为真理而战的坚毅身影。

"Who compares with a slender pen? Mauser has three thousand elite soldiers." These lines from Chairman Mao Zedong's "Lin Jiang Xian" find their most vivid interpretation here in Hexi Village, Wu'an. In the summer of 1946, the People's Daily of Jin-Ji-Lu-Yu Border Region and the Jin-Ji-Lu-Yu regional head office of Xinhua News Agency merged operations on this site. Every pen here transformed into a steel rifle aimed directly at the enemy's heart.

Stepping into the courtyard, it feels as if time rewinds to those war-torn days: editors writing furiously by sesame-oil lamp, typesetters selecting characters in a converted temple workshop, militia guarding the printing caves. Here, they created a miracle of red journalism, making the Jinjiluyu edition of the *People's Daily* a powerful voice of the times. Equally moving are the stories of legacy and mentorship: pioneering journalists like Wang Chun (1907–1951) and Zhang Panshi (1905–2000), who under fire not only chronicled history but also nurtured the first generation of red media workers for New China. Today, as sunlight filters through the lattice windows of this courtyard, one can still faintly hear the crisp clatter of lead type being set and catch glimpses of those resolute figures who fought for truth as their weapon.

06

到山底村，探寻"地下长城"的烽火记忆
Venture into Shandi Village to Discover the Beacon Memories of the "Underground Great Wall"

峰峰矿区的山底村，太行山脚下这个看似普通的村落，竟藏着两段"硬核"历史。南宋时期，岳飞抗金大军在此激战，百姓为避金兵挖出"躲金洞"，堪称古代版"地道战"的雏形。七百年后，面对日寇铁蹄，村民们把祖传的"土遁术"升级——用镐头和簸箕挖出了抗战地道网，妥妥的"民间基建狂魔"。

躬身进入狭窄的地道入口，仿佛叩开了时空之门。这座"地下长城"将寻常村落化为要塞：灶台藏射击孔，驴槽设暗哨，水井隐通道，处处闪耀着军民们的智慧。双层地道自成体系，防水防毒更可歼敌；精巧的"翻板陷阱"，令日寇哀叹"如坠迷魂阵"。这不仅是防御工事，更是用生命铸就的抗战丰碑，见证了邯郸人民的勇气与智慧。

　　At Shandi Village in Fengfeng Mining District, this seemingly ordinary village at the foot of the Taihang Mountains conceals two segments of "hard-core" history! During the Southern Song Dynasty (1127–1279), Yue Fei's anti-Jin forces fought fiercely here, and villagers dug a "gold-hiding cave" to escape the Jin's invasion—an early prototype of Chinese "tunnel warfare." Seven hundred years later, facing the Japanese invaders, villagers upgraded their ancestral "earth escape techniques"—using pickaxes and dustpans to excavate one tunnel networks built during the War of Resistance Against Japanese Aggression. Truly "grassroots infrastructure giant."

　　Bending to enter the narrow, one-square-meter tunnel entrance feels like unlocking a door through time. This "Underground Great Wall" transformed a humble village into a fortress: stoves concealed gun ports, donkey troughs hid sentry points, and well walls masked escape tunnels. Everywhere you look, the wisdom of the people and soldiers shines through. The double-layered tunnel system was fully self-contained: waterproof, gas-resistant, and enemy-repelling. Ingenious "flip-board traps" made Japanese invaders lament, "Entering Shandi Village feels like falling into a phantom maze." More than a defense structure, it is a monument carved by life and death for the War of Resistance Against Japanese Aggression, testifying to the courage and ingenuity of the people of Handan.

07

探访直南党史馆，寻找那束照亮前路的光
Trace the Light That Illuminated the Path at Zhinan County Party Revolution Museum

　　谁说革命史就得板着脸？来磁县直南党史馆看看，这里的九个"第一"简直就是在"秀优越"：直南第一个共产党员、第一个中共支部、第一个党小组……

　　走进展馆，历史瞬间"活"了：1922年冬，李大钊与王子清执手相握，定格"铁肩担道义"的永恒瞬间；1925年直南第一个党支部成立时的油灯尚明，1937年磁县抗日民主县政府选举的掌声犹在耳畔。最燃的是直南特委活动沙盘，红色箭头勾勒出革命火种如何在冀南豫北鲁西蔓延。这哪是党史馆，分明是一部立体的红色记忆簿。那些围巾传递的温暖、油灯照亮的誓言，都在诉说着：信仰的温度，永远不会随时间的流逝而冷却。

Who says revolutionary history has to be solemn? Come to the Zhinan County Party History Museum in Cixian County to see nine "firsts" on full display—Zhinan's first CPC member, first CPC branch, first Party group...

Walking into the museum, history instantly "comes alive": in winter 1922, Li Dazhao (1889–1927) and Wang Ziqing (1903–1938) clasp hands—an enduring image of "iron shoulders bearing moral duty." The oil lamp marking the 1925 founding of Zhinan's first CPC branch still burns, and you can almost hear the applause from the 1937 election of Cixian County's first anti-Japanese democratic county government. The most thrilling is the interactive sand-table: red arrows trace how revolutionary sparks spread through southern Hebei, northern Henan, and western Shandong. This isn't just a Party history museum—it's a vivid red memory album. Those scarves passing warmth and the oath lit by oil lamps silently declare: the warmth of belief never cools with the passage of time.

磁县陶泉乡花驼村 · Huatuo Village, Taoquan Township, Cixian County

到花驼村，解锁抗战时期的"云端"兵工厂
Visit Huatuo Village to Discover a "Cloud-Based" Arsenal from the War of Resistance Against Japanese Aggression

海拔七百米的花驼村，这个被称作"天尖村"的古村落，妥妥是抗战时期的"军工天花板"，八路军一二九师在此秘密建立了华北地区重要的军工基地。

走进由石砌民房改建的兵工厂博物馆，仿佛打开了时光隧道。机床静静陈列，手工打磨的步枪枪管依然泛着冷光，唐代石碾上残留的火药痕迹都在无声述说着那段"没有枪没有炮，我们自己造"的燃情岁月。站在天保寨俯瞰全村，山风掠过，仿佛还能听见当年锻造枪械的铿锵之声，看见村民们连夜赶制军需的忙碌身影。

Perched at an elevation of 700 meters, Huatuo Village, known locally as "Village at the Tip of the Sky," was indisputably the "military-industrial pinnacle" of its time. The 129th Division of the Eighth Route Army secretly established a vital weapons production base in North China here.

Step into the Arsenal Museum, transformed from traditional stone-built dwellings, and it feels as though you've entered a time tunnel. Lathes stand silently in place, and the cold gleam of hand-polished rifle barrels still lingers. Even the traces of gunpowder on a Tang Dynasty stone mill silently recount those fiery years when "without guns or cannons, we built our own." From the hilltop Tianbao Fort, look down upon the entire village—let the mountain winds carry echoes of clanging metals from days when firearms were forged here, and catch the sight of villagers working through the night to supply the frontlines.

09

石榴花下多奇志，不爱红妆爱武装
Beneath the Pomegranate Blossoms, A Woman of Valor Who Chose Arms Over Adornment

大名县金滩镇的青砖院落里，革命的火种在此点燃——这里是邯郸女杰郭隆真从觉醒走向不朽的起点。

正是在这里，年仅十五岁的郭隆真和父亲一同创办了大名县第一所女子学堂。这位民国时期的"独立女性"，此后成长为出色的妇女运动领导人之一。她曾与周恩来、邓颖超共同创办觉悟社，在革命史上留下重要印记。如今，最令人动容的是院中那棵百年石榴树——相传是郭隆真幼年所植，至今仍灼灼其华，恰似她炽热的革命理想。站在郭隆真断然拒婚的闺房前，那句临刑前的誓言犹在耳畔："宁可牺牲，绝不屈节！"

Step into the gray-brick courtyard in Jintan Town, Daming County, and you'll find the birthplace of a revolutionary spark, the place where Guo Longzhen (1894–1931), the remarkable Handan heroine, first awakened and set out on the path to immortality.

It was here that, at just 15 years old, Guo Longzhen co-founded Daming County's first school for girls with her father. This trailblazing "independent woman" during the Republic of China period would later rise to become a prominent leader in the women's movement. She co-founded the Awakening Society alongside Zhou Enlai and Deng Yingchao (1904–1992), leaving an indelible mark on the history of the revolution. Today, the most moving relic may be the hundred-year-old pomegranate tree in the courtyard—said to have been planted by Guo herself in childhood. It still blooms brightly, just like her fiery revolutionary ideals. Standing before the room where she once resolutely refused an arranged marriage, one can almost hear her defiant words before execution: "I would rather die than yield!"

10

漫步伯延，重温周恩来的"四个昼夜"
Walk Through Boyan to Trace Footsteps Left by Zhou Enlai in Four Days and Nights

　　车过武安城南，伯延古镇的青砖灰瓦在太行余脉的怀抱中渐次浮现。这座明清时期的商帮重镇，曾见证无数车马辐辏的辉煌。1961 年，这座古镇迎来了一位特殊的客人。周恩来总理走进伯延古镇的街巷院落，用四天四夜倾听百姓心声，在这里留下了珍贵足迹。如今，漫步街巷，仍能感受到那份真挚的为民情怀——在召开座谈会的大院，在走访过的供销社旧址，在老槐树下与农民的促膝长谈中，处处书写着共产党人"从群众中来，到群众中去"的鲜活注脚。

　　今日的伯延，既是明清时期的文化古镇，更是共产党人践行群众路线的精神地标。在这里，让我们在青砖黛瓦间触摸明清商脉，在红色记忆中体悟初心使命。

South of Wu'an lies Boyan Ancient Town, where its blue bricks and gray tiles gradually emerged, cradled within the arms of the Taihang Mountains. Once a bustling commercial hub during the Ming and Qing dynasties, Boyan witnessed the clamor of caravans and traders. In 1961, this historic town welcomed a very special guest: Premier Zhou Enlai (1898–1976). Over the course of four full days and nights, he walked its streets and courtyards, listening intently to the voices of ordinary people and leaving behind precious footprints of his visit. Even today, wandering these streets evokes a deep sense of his heartfelt dedication to the people, whether in the courtyard where he held forums, at the former supply and marketing cooperative he visited, or under the old pagoda tree where he sat in close conversation with farmers. Each location vividly illustrates the Communist ideal of "from the masses, to the masses."

Modern-day Boyan stands as both a cultural relic of the Ming and Qing dynasties and a spiritual landmark where the CPC members practiced the Mass Line. Here, one can trace the commercial veins of ancient China while also rediscovering the Party's original mission through red memory.

成安县道东堡镇道东堡村润翔路东段 · East Segment of Runxiang Road, Daodongbu Village, Daodongbu Town, Cheng'an County

到成安红色文化园，追寻毛主席棉田视察的温暖足迹

Visit Cheng'an Red Culture Park and Follow Chairman Mao's Warm Footsteps in the Cotton Fields

成安，藏着一个有故事的红色文化园。1959年9月24日，这里迎来了毛泽东主席。毛主席在这里视察了成安万亩丰产棉田，与群众进行了亲切交谈。如今，文化园以光影、场景与老照片还原当年情景，让这场跨越六十余年的"伟人遇见"焕发鲜活温度。

漫步园区，仿佛能听到主席爽朗的笑声回荡田间。乘602路公交返程时，晚风轻拂车窗，远处棉絮如云，恍若历史的余温仍在心间流淌。这不仅是成安的"红色地标"，更是一场沉浸式红色记忆之旅，让人触摸到领袖与人民之间最朴素深厚的情谊。

Cheng'an holds a Red Culture Park steeped in stories of legacy. On September 24, 1959, it welcomed its most iconic guest, Chairman Mao Zedong, who came to inspect the high-yield cotton fields covering tens of thousands of *mu*. He warmly engaged with the local farmers during his visit. Today, the park uses light, sound, and historical photographs to vividly recreate scenes from that visit, letting this encounter with the great man, which has spanned over six decades, regain its vitality and warmth.

As you stroll through the park, you can almost hear Chairman Mao Zedong's hearty laughter echoing through the fields. On your return journey aboard Bus Route 602, the evening breeze brushes the windows, distant cotton tufts float like clouds, and the lingering warmth of history fills the heart. This is more than a "red landmark" of Cheng'an. It's an immersive journey into red memory, one that brings to life the deep, unadorned bond between the people and their leader.

丛台区中华北大街 515 号 · No. 515 Zhonghua North Street, Congtai District

12

寻访"时光站台"，倾听车轮上的国家故事
Visit the "Time Platform" and Listen to the Nation's Story on Steel Wheels

在河北司法警官职业学校葱郁的林间，锈迹斑驳的铁轨静静延伸，这里曾是共和国最特别的"移动办公室"——毛主席专列的历史停靠点。1952 至 1974 年间，这趟载着共和国蓝图的列车二十六次经停邯郸。毛泽东主席九次开启车门深入调研，二十次在车厢里听取各省市汇报。如今，斑驳的枕木间依稀可辨当年警卫战士的脚印，风过树梢的沙沙声里，仿佛还回荡着专列到站时的汽笛长鸣。不远处，棉纺厂的老工人们至今仍会指着专线轨道，讲述领袖接见纺织工人的温暖瞬间。这是一个永远停留在时光里的红色站台，等待着每一代人来倾听那些车轮上的国家故事。

Tucked beneath the lush canopy of trees at the Hebei Vocational College for Correctional Police lies a rusted stretch of railway track—once the nation's most unique "mobile office." This was a regular stop for Chairman Mao Zedong's special train. Between 1952 and 1974, the train, carrying the blueprint of the People's Republic of China, made 26 stops in Handan. He stepped

off the train 9 times to conduct in-depth field investigations and held 20 briefings inside the train cars to hear reports from various provinces and municipalities. Even today, the faded wooden ties bear faint traces of the guards who once paced their length. In the gentle rustle of wind through the treetops, you might still hear the whistle of that legendary train. Nearby, veteran workers from the local textile mill still point to the tracks as they recount the touching moment when Chairman Mao Zedong met with textile workers. This is a "red platform" forever frozen in time, inviting each new generation to listen to the nation's stories carried on the wheels.

13

仰望跃峰渠，膜拜穿越山岭的"人工天河"
Behold the Yuefeng Canal and Worship the "Man-Made Heavenly River" Carved Through Mountain Peaks

　　跃峰渠，人类硬扛太行的"人工天河"神作！20世纪70年代，一群建设者抡锤扛锹，在悬崖峭壁间"绣"出这条生命水脉，硬把漳河水"拽"进干渴的冀南大地——万顷田地秒变水润"绿宝石"！

　　跃峰渠核心担当要属险峰渡槽，"亚洲第一单跨石拱"绝非虚名，210米身板横跨双峰，单孔跨度106米惊掉下巴！最绝的是这里是用2.6万余块精度误差不超过两毫米的石头"码"成的。仰望槽身悬于深渊，激流轰鸣在山谷"打碟"，分分钟腿软又上头！

　　如今这里成了红色课堂，老建设者的故事代代流传，年轻人摸着凿痕累累的工具，读懂了什么是"自力更生、艰苦奋斗"。它流的哪里是水？分明是石头缝里蹦出的"勇气"和"智慧"。每一道浪花都在喊：看！这就是前辈用血肉刻下的"硬核浪漫"，更是要代代相传的精神密码！

The Yuefeng Canal is a human-engineered marvel, a "man-made heavenly river" that navigates on the formidable Taihang Mountains. In the 1970s, a team of determined builders wielded hammers and shovels, and "embroidered" this lifeline through perilous cliffs, forcefully channeling the Zhanghe River's waters into the parched lands of southern Hebei, turning tens of thousands of hectares of dry farmland into emerald fields at lightning speed.

The Yaofeng Aqueduct stands as the pivotal feature the Yuefeng Canal. The title of "Asia's largest single-span stone arch" is no exaggeration. This 210-meter-long structure spans twin peaks

with a jaw-dropping single-arch span of 106 meters. The most astonishing part? It was built using over 26,000 stones, each with a margin of error under 2 millimeters. Look up at the aqueduct, suspended above the abyss, while the torrent roars through the valley like a DJ spinning a mountain beat. It'll leave your legs trembling and your heart racing!

Today, this site serves as a classroom of red heritage. The stories of old builders are passed down through generations. Young visitors, running their hands over the battered tools, come to grasp the true meaning of "self-reliance and hard work." What flows here is not just water. It's a surge of "courage" and "wisdom" born from stone. Every splash cries out—Look! This is the "hardcore romance" carved by our predecessors with blood and sweat, and it's a spiritual code meant to be passed on forever.

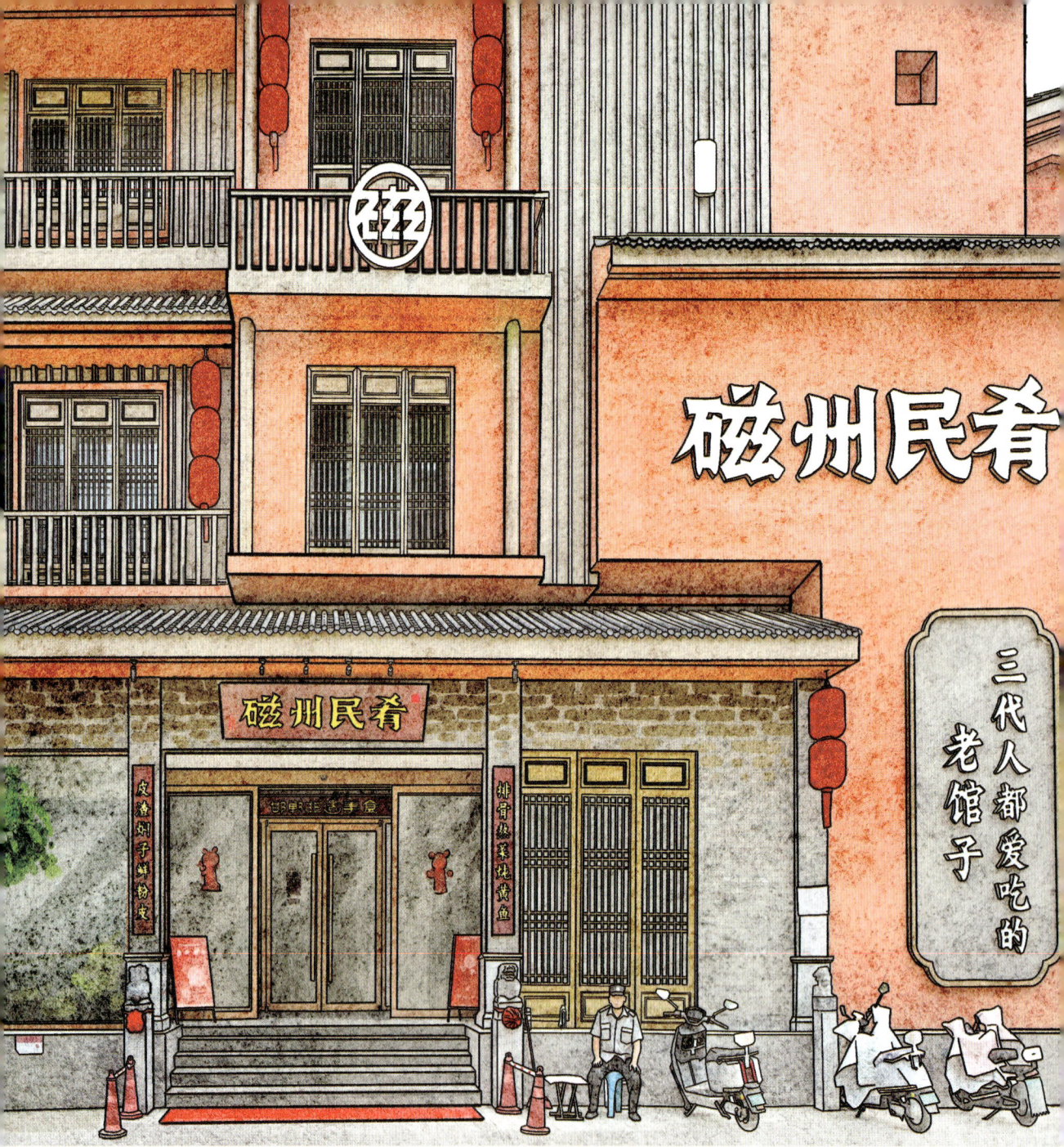

来邯郸的餐桌玩一场"穿越"吧！赵都礼宴把战国故事端上桌，春满园的成语宴让你边吃边"涨知识"，咬一口永年驴肉香肠，撕一只二毛烧鸡，再吸溜一碗红豆焖罐面，连花馍都长得像艺术品！三千年的烟火气，全藏在这一口口香喷喷的惊喜里了。

Get ready to "time travel" via Handan's dining table! The Zhao Capital Banquet brings tales from the Warring States Period straight to your plate. At Chunmanyuan Restaurant, the Idiom Banquet lets you savor both flavors and knowledge with every bite. Sink your teeth into Yongnian's donkey sausage, tear into a glistening Ermao Roast Chicken, and slurp down a bowl of red bean clay-pot noodles. Even the *huamo* look like edible works of art! Every fragrant, mouthwatering bite is steeped in the essence of three thousand years of culinary tradition.

一口吃掉三千年

A Bite Through Three Thousand Years

品赵都礼宴，用一顿饭的时间穿越到战国
Experience the Zhao Capital Banquet and Travel to the Warring States in a Single Meal

当暮色降临邯郸，赵都礼宴的大门缓缓开启，一场穿越时空的文化之旅正徐徐展开。身着战国袍的侍者温文尔雅，错落有致的战国建筑高台厚榭，卷轴式样的菜单精妙绝伦，三足青铜爵中琼浆微漾……此刻执爵而立的您，恍惚间恰似那邯郸道上赴赵王夜宴的列国诸侯，广角镜头定格处，分明是一幅"诸侯临朝"的战国帛画。随着乐声响起，九道佳肴与九个节目次第登场。《完璧归赵》配以琥珀炆玉环，和氏璧造型的菜品在灯光下熠熠生辉；压轴的太极八卦椰奶冻秀出阴阳相济，完美诠释着刚柔并济的古老哲思。

觥筹交错时，青铜冰鉴透出的凉意轻触指尖，忽然懂得这座三千年古城最动人的秘密——它将青铜器上的饕餮纹化作盘中风景，让竹简里的刀笔刻痕变成唇间故事。离席时风动帷帐，窗外丛台灯火与天上星河交错，而齿颊间徘徊的赵酒醇香，早已将这段邯郸记忆酿成了属于您的"赵都礼宴"。

As dusk falls over Handan, the grand gate of the Zhao Capital Banquet slowly opens, and a cultural journey through time quietly begins. Attendants in elegant Warring States-style robes greet you with grace; elevated halls and tiered platforms reflect ancient architecture; the scroll-style menu is a work of art; and the fine liquor in your three-legged bronze *jue* vessel ripples gently… In that moment, cup in hand, you might well imagine yourself a noble guest on Handandao, attending a royal banquet with the King of Zhao. Freeze this scene through a wide-angle lens, and it becomes a live-action silk painting from the Warring States: "Lords at Court." As music plays, nine courses and nine performances unfold in turn. The performance "Returning the Jade Intact to Zhao" is served alongside the dish "Amber-Braised Jade Rings," its presentation inspired by the *He Shi Bi* (a Warring States-era ceremonial jade) glowing brilliantly under the

lights. The grand finale, the Tai Chi Yin-Yang Coconut Milk Jelly, perfectly embodies the ancient philosophy of balance between softness and strength.

In the clinking of bronze vessels, the cool touch of an ice bucket grazes your fingertips, and suddenly you understand the most enchanting secret of this 3,000-year-old city: it transforms the *taotie* motifs on bronze ware into plated artistry and turns bamboo-slip inscriptions into stories told on the tongue. As you leave, the wind rustles the curtains; outside, the lights of Congtai Platform mingle with the stars above. And lingering on your palate, the mellow fragrance of Zhao wine has already distilled your experience into a personal memory of the Zhao Capital Banquet.

02

打卡邯郸必吃榜！春满园才是隐藏的文化美食王者

Check off Handan's Must-Eat Chunmanyuan Restaurant Where Every Bite Reveals a Cultural Story

　　朋友们，来邯郸别只知道吃驴肉火烧了！春满园直接把三千年古都的饮食文化端上桌——进门就被汉服小姐姐整破防了，上菜还带讲历史故事的，吃饭秒变文化课！

　　你看，武安小米羊肉焖饭堪称一绝，精选武安特产的黄金小米，与羊肉、胡萝卜、豌豆苗慢火焖制，米香与肉香完美融合，既保留了传统风味，又增添了现代营养理念。四扣碗更是匠心独运：腐乳肉、酥肉、海带、豆腐两荤两素，搭配荷叶饼食用，层次丰富，回味无穷，一口穿越回战国。最令人称绝的是餐厅打造的"成语宴"。"完璧归赵"以冬瓜为璧，仙贝为饰，鱼子酱点缀，将历史典故完美呈现于盘中，拍照发圈直接被问爆！连酸奶杯都写着成语，喝个酸奶都能"涨知识"，这波文化输出我服！

　　Foodies, if you're coming to Handan, don't stop at donkey burgers! Chunmanyuan takes the culinary culture of this 3,000-year-old ancient capital and serves it right to your table. Step inside and you'll be greeted by hostesses in Hanfu—instant culture shock in the best way. Each dish comes with a story, turning your meal into a live history lesson.

　　Take the Wu'an millet and lamb clay-pot rice. It's an absolute gem. Made with golden millet native to Wu'an, slow-cooked with tender lamb, carrots, and pea shoots, the dish masterfully balances traditional flavors with modern nutrition. Even more ingenious is the "four-compartment bowl" set: fermented tofu pork, braised crispy pork, kelp, and tofu, two meat and two vegetable sides, served with lotus leaf pancakes. Rich in layers and flavor, it's a bite-sized journey back to the Warring States. The showstopper, though, is the restaurant's "Idiom Banquet." For example, "Returning the Jade Intact to Zhao" is interpreted as a dish with winter melon carved like jade, garnished with rice crackers and caviar, bringing the historical idiom to life on the plate. Post it online and get ready to be bombarded with questions! Even the yogurt cups are printed with idioms. You'll leave not only with a full stomach, but also a full brain! Cultural export? Nailed it.

03

来永年，赴一场与驴肉香肠的"百年之约"
Head to Yongnian for a "Century-Old Date" with Donkey Sausage

"天上龙肉，地下驴肉！"这句民间俗语直接把驴肉捧上美食神坛——龙肉是传说，但驴肉可是实打实的鲜嫩香醇！尤其在邯郸，不吃一顿永年驴肉香肠，等于白来！（偷偷告诉你，比网红牛排更让人上头。）这道传承百年的美食是邯郸妥妥的"美食圈顶流"！

走进老作坊，师傅们正将精驴肉化作红白相间的肉糜，加上绿豆淀粉和小磨香油，配上祖传的香料方子，灌入天然肠衣，这波操作堪称"永年米其林秘方"。别问"好不好吃"，一千个人心里藏着一千张叛逆的味蕾地图，只管来就对了！老街巷口，刚出锅的香肠在案板上微微颤动，老师傅的刀起落间，薄如蝉翼的切片透出琥珀般的肌理。隔壁现打的烧饼裹着滚烫香肠，芝麻的焦香与果木烟熏味在空气中缠绵，金黄的芝麻油顺着焦脆的饼皮缓缓流淌。这座古城三千年的饮食智慧，都浓缩在这简单却极致的美味里。打卡台词都替你想好了——"在邯郸实现驴肉自由，龙肉吃不到，但这一口赢了！"

"Dragon meat in the sky, donkey meat on earth!" This folk saying puts donkey meat at the top of the food pyramid. Dragon meat may be myth, but donkey meat is the real deal: tender, savory, and unforgettable. Especially in Handan, where missing out on Yongnian's donkey sausage is practically sacrilegious. (Insider tip: it's even more addictive than trending steak joints!) This culinary treasure, passed down for over a century, is a certified top-tier dish in Handan's foodie circles.

Step into an old workshop and watch the masters at work: finely minced donkey meat, red and white marbled, is blended with mung bean starch, fragrant sesame oil,

and a secret family spice mix, then encased in natural sausage skins. This process is basically the "Michelin recipe of Yongnian." Don't ask "Is it good?"—with a thousand rebellious taste buds mapping a thousand cravings, just come and find out! At the corner of an old alleyway, freshly steamed sausages quiver on the cutting board. With every precise slice, thin as cicada wings, their amber marbling gleams. Nearby, sesame flatbreads are stuffed with piping hot sausage. The toasty sesame aroma mingle with woodsmoke in the air, and golden sesame oil slowly seep into the crispy crust. In this one simple yet masterful bite, the culinary wisdom of three millennia is condensed. We've even got your foodie caption ready: "Achieved donkey meat freedom in Handan—can't eat dragon meat, but this bite wins!"

04

徒手撕二毛烧鸡，汤汁沾满手才是对祖传卤味的最高礼仪
Tear Apart Ermao Roast Chicken Where Sauce-Stained Fingers Are the Highest Tribute to Ancestral Marinades

"想吃鸡得跑快腿，吃了以后得捂住嘴"，大名府这句老话说的正是传承两百年的二毛烧鸡。这只从嘉庆年间"飞"来的非遗美味，藏着让人欲罢不能的玄机。十几味名贵中药在老汤里修炼百年，砂仁醒脾、肉桂温阳，暗合《本草纲目》的食补智慧。每当日头西斜，那口沉淀着岁月的老汤便开始在铸铁锅中轻声絮语，将时光的厚度一寸寸渗入鸡肉肌理。若赶上清晨出锅，不妨学本地人拎着油纸包边走边啃，任肉香招惹半条街的馋虫。末了别忘了嗦嗦手指——那抹粘连指尖的胶质，可是两百年手艺的美味印章。

下班了，买上一份二毛烧鸡、五百居香肠和郭八烧饼，自制"汉堡"，邯郸人津津乐道的"二五八套餐"这不就有了。

"If you want chicken, you've got to run fast. Once you eat it, don't let the word out!" This old saying from Daming Prefecture refers to the irresistible allure of the Ermao Roast Chicken, a delicacy passed down for over 200 years. Originating in the Jiaqing reign (1796–1820) of the Qing Dynasty, this intangible heritage dish hides addictive secrets. A dozen precious medicinal herbs steep for centuries in the old broth: amomum to awaken the spleen, cinnamon for warmth—wisdom rooted in *Compendium of Materia Medica*. Every evening, as the sun dips low, the broth whispers in cast-iron cauldrons, time soaking into the very fibers of the chicken. Catch it

early in the morning, fresh from the pot, and do as the locals do: grab a paper-wrapped parcel and munch as you walk. The aroma alone is enough to awaken cravings up and down the street. Don't forget to lick your fingers at the end—that sticky collagen clinging to your fingertips? It's the flavor stamp of 200 years of culinary mastery.

Off work, grab Handan's unique trinity—Ermao Roast Chicken, Wubai ju Sausage, Guoba Bread—stack them up for the iconic "258 Burger" locals can't stop hyping!

0 5

品五百居香肠，体验山东厨神在大名留下的 "五百里风味"

Savor Wubai Ju Sausage, Where a Shandong Master Left Five Hundred Li of Flavor in Daming

五百居一出手就是"降维打击"——1821 年，山东厨神王湘云在大名道开了家店，因为离济南约五百里，干脆取名"五百居"。这根香肠，直接把济南府的风味和大名府的物产"锁死"在肠衣里，成了"美食活化石"。

老字号玩起"时光魔法"来简直得心应手：精选的猪后腿肉按"六瘦四肥"的黄金比例，加入砂仁、桂楠等香料"天团"，再灌进肠衣里"闭关修炼"。成品切开那刻直接"美颜暴击"——琥珀色的肉冻闪着油光。咬下去肉香就在嘴里"炸街"，越嚼越上头。最绝的是这肠子自带"防腐"效果，大夏天都不带坏的。所以"灵魂拷问"来了，这根让邯郸人骄傲了两百年的香肠，你不想来尝一尝吗？

When Wubai Ju steps into the ring, it's game over for the competition. In 1821, the legendary Shandong chef Wang Xiangyun opened a shop in Daming Circuit, roughly 500 *li* (about 250 kilometers) from Jinan, Shandong Province, hence the name "Wubai Ju," or "The 500-Li House." His sausages fused the essence of Jinan cuisine with the bounty of Daming, creating a true "culinary fossil."

When it comes to "time-bending flavor," this old brand is a master: premium pork hindquarters are trimmed to a "60 lean/40 fat" golden ratio, blended with a superstar lineup of spices, amomum, cinnamon camphor, and more, then sealed into sausage casings for "closed-door cultivation." Cut into one and you get an instant beauty filter: amber-colored meat jelly glistens with oil. One bite, and flavor explodes in your mouth. The more you chew, the better it gets. Best part? These sausages have built-in "preservation power." They don't spoil even in the peak of summer. So here comes the real question—This sausage that's made Handan proud for 200 years. Don't you want to try it for yourself?

06

大名县大名府路与元城街交叉口西行 100 米路南 · 100 meters west from the intersection of Damingfu Road and Yuancheng Street, south side of the road, Daming County

咬一口郭八火烧，让麦香和芝麻香在舌尖翻跟头
Take a Bite of Guoba Huoshao and Let the Aroma of Wheat and Sesame Tumble on Your Tongue

"咔嚓——"这声脆响，是大名人刻在基因里的美食暗号！清晨的街角，正上演着面食界的"功夫大片"：面团在案板上翻飞摔打，每道褶皱都藏着祖传的力道密码。当火烧跳进祖传耐石鏊子的那一刻，麦香混着芝麻香，瞬间"攻陷"整条街巷。

这可不是普通碳水——二十五层薄如蝉翼的面皮，在老师傅手下驯服地叠成"千层雪"。耐石炙烤出的金黄外壳会"唱歌"，咬下去是酥脆、柔韧、咸香的三重暴击。老饕们最懂行：趁热切开，塞满五百居香肠、卤蛋、卤豆腐，让面香与肉香在口腔里上演"神仙打架"。"宁可三日无肉，不可一日无火烧！"大名人把对面食的痴狂，都揉进了这掌心大的美味里。

Crunch!—that crisp crackle is a code hardwired into every Daming native's foodie DNA. On a morning street corner, a full-blown culinary action scene is underway: dough leaps and spins on the counter, each fold stamped with generations of practiced strength. As the *huoshao* (literally "crispy baked flatbread") hits the seasoned stone griddle, the scent of toasted wheat and sesame instantly captures the whole street.

But this isn't your average carb bomb—25 layers of dough, thin as cicada wings, are folded into a snowy mille-feuille. The golden crust, seared by fire-hardened stone, sizzles and sings. Bite into it, and a triple impact of crisp, chewy, and savory hits you all at once. True gourmets know the secret: slice it open while hot and stuff it with Wubai Ju sausage, soy-braised eggs, or marinated tofu. In that moment, wheat and meat collide in a flavor battle of the gods. "Better to go three days without meat than a single day without *huoshao*." Every Daming local folds their passion for dough into this palm-sized masterpiece.

07

磁州民肴 2.0，老邯郸的胃满足了新世代的嘴
Try Cizhou Folk Cuisine 2.0, Where Old Handan Flavors Meet Modern Tastebuds

　　老字号也有新玩法。推开那幢雕花木门，扑面而来的是老磁州带着创新味的烟火气！这家磁州民肴可不简单——千岛湖的鱼头泡着邯郸的馍，生焗虾球都带着赵都的江湖气。"外地的食材，邯郸的魂！"创始人张国庆正给鱼头泡馍加冕"一帅"——这碗现炖的浓汤撞上金黄馍块，哪还有半点儿"黑乎乎"的老印象？再看那"九将"天团：磁州焖子带着冬奥会的荣光，地锅鸡在辣椒丛里"撒野"……

　　"咱邯郸菜啊，就像回车巷的典故——"服务员笑道，"看着规矩，内里可藏着混搭的智慧！"这里连开餐词都是文化"大拌菜"。要问什么最下饭？当然是这一桌"非遗"级的创新，因为能让千岛湖鱼头说出邯郸话的，全城独此一家！

Time-honored brands are finding fresh ways to shine. Push open the carved wooden door and be greeted by the sizzling aromas of old Cizhou blended with the flair of modern creativity. This isn't just any Cizhou-style restaurant. Here, Thousand-Island Lake fish heads are simmered with Handan's signature flatbread, and even baked shrimp balls carry the bold aura of the then Zhao capital's culinary swagger. "Ingredients from afar, soul from Handan!" says founder Zhang Guoqing, as he ceremoniously crowns the fish head and flatbread dish as the "Commander of the Banquet." That day's freshly simmered golden broth meets golden buns, banishing any trace of the old "murky" stereotype. Then comes the "Nine Generals" lineup: Cizhou-style menzi (fried starch cakes) carrying the pride of the Winter Olympics, and ground pot chicken going wild in a forest of chilies...

"Our Handan cuisine," a smiling server explains, "is just like the old story of Huiche Lane: proper on the outside, but packed with clever fusion inside!" Even the meal's opening toast is a cultural

potluck: before the final words of the slogan "So close, so beautiful, spend your weekends in Hebei" have landed, guests are already snapping photos of the idiom-themed banquet with their phones. What's the best dish to go with rice? Undoubtedly, this spread of intangible heritage-level innovation. After all, where else can you hear a Thousand-Island fish head speak fluent Handan?

08

来尝一尝红豆焖罐面，看面在陶罐里跳圆舞曲
Try the Red Bean Slow-Simmered Noodles and Watch Them Waltz in a Clay Pot

　　"咕嘟——咕嘟——"街角的餐馆里，陶土罐正上演着"高温桑拿秀"：手工抻面在秘制红豆骨汤里翻滚舒展，每根面条都吸饱了汤汁的"精髓"。吃法也有讲究：先喝口原汤唤醒味蕾，再拌上辣油和香醋，让甜、咸、辣在舌尖"三足鼎立"。

　　邯郸人对红豆焖罐面的执着，超乎你的想象。从清晨赶工的工人到深夜下班的职员，谁不是被这罐热气治愈了疲惫？如今，它依然是街头最暖的烟火气——毕竟，有什么忧愁是一罐红豆焖面抚平不了的呢？如果不行，那就再加个卤蛋吧！

Gudu—gudu... From a street-corner restaurant comes the sound of bubbling. Clay pots are putting on a "high-heat sauna show." Hand-pulled noodles stretch and swirl in a secret red bean and bone broth, each strand soaking up the essence of the soup. There's a method to enjoying this dish: first, sip the original broth to awaken your taste buds; then mix in chili oil and aromatic vinegar, letting sweetness, saltiness, and spiciness form a "tripod of flavors" on your tongue.

Handan people's love for red bean clay pot noodles goes beyond what you might expect. From early-rising workers to late-shift employees, who hasn't had their weariness soothed by a steaming bowl of this goodness? Even today, it remains one of the warmest comforts on the street. After all, what sorrow can't be eased by a bowl of red bean noodles? And if not, just add a marinated egg—problem solved!

09

丛台区丛台路与广泰街交叉口西行 20 米路北禾麦新语花馍店 475 号商铺，Shop No. 475, Hemai Xinyu Flower Bun Store, 20 meters west of the intersection of Congtai Road and Guangtai Street, north side of the road, Congtai District

吃邯郸花馍，见证老面馒头变身舌尖上的艺术品
Eat a Handan Huamo and Witness How a Steamed Bun Becomes Edible Art

在邯郸，花馍可不是普通的馒头，而是能吃的"手办"！老一辈用白面捏成小羊送给晚辈，寓意吉祥；如今的花馍还玩出了新花样——菠菜汁染绿"树叶"，苋菜汁晕出粉红花瓣，甚至还能定制金腰带造型（没错，张伟丽同款）！

花馍制作的传承人将老手艺"卷"出了新高度：五颜六色的花馍花束，圆润可爱的寿桃，憨态可掬的兔子，排列整齐的枣山等，各式各样的花馍充满了美好寓意。从"蒸锅里的祝福"到"朋友圈打卡神器"，邯郸花馍靠着果蔬"调色盘"和"脑洞大开"的馅料，愣是把传统民俗变成了年轻人的心头好。毕竟，谁能拒绝一个又好看又能啃的"艺术品"呢？

In Handan, *huamo* (flower-shaped steamed buns) aren't just steamed buns. They're edible figurines! In the past, elders shaped white flour into lambs to gift younger generations, symbols of good fortune. Today, *huamo* artistry has evolved: spinach juice dyes leaf patterns green, amaranth brings out pink petals, and you can even order a golden championship belt design (yes, just like that of the UFC champion Zhang Weili)!

The inheritors of *huamo* craftsmanship have taken this traditional skill to new heights: vibrant floral bouquets, chubby birthday peaches, charming rabbits, and neat rows of jujube-studded buns—each one imbued with heartfelt symbolism.

From "blessings in a steamer" to "social media darlings," Handan *huamo* use natural fruit and vegetable colors and wildly imaginative fillings to transform folk tradition into something beloved by younger generations. Let's be honest: who could resist an "art piece" that's both beautiful and biteable?

品广府酥鱼，尝一口千年不散的江湖味
Bite Guangfu Crispy Fish and Let the Jianghu Flavor Transport You Through a Thousand Years

宋海饭店后厨，老师傅正施展着独门绝技：精选的鲜活鲫鱼在秘制老汤中慢炖六小时，鱼骨软如酥糖，鱼肉却还保持着迷人的纹理。这火候的掌控，比武侠小说里的内功心法还要精妙三分。

上桌时，鱼身完整如艺术品，筷子轻触即瞬间化开。入口的刹那，先是一缕陈醋的醇香扑鼻而来，接着是老汤的鲜美层层绽放，最后是鱼肉的甘甜在舌尖萦绕。就凭这滋味，广府酥鱼想上《舌尖上的中国》不过分吧？！

窗外的古城墙默默点赞：从街坊四邻的"下饭神器"，到美食博主的"流量密码"，这道酥鱼始终保持着让手机先吃的觉悟。难怪网友戏称："广府酥鱼，连鱼刺都是戏精——又酥又戏多！"

Step into the kitchen of Songhai Restaurant and you'll see the master chef performing his signature move: fresh carp, carefully selected, is slow-simmered in a secret aged broth for six hours. The bones soften to the texture of sugar candy, while the flesh retains its exquisite texture. This precise control of heat is more refined than the inner power in a martial arts novel.

When served, the fish arrives whole like a work of art, yet it melts at the lightest touch of chopsticks. With the first bite, the aroma of aged vinegar rises, followed by the rich layers of the broth, and finally the delicate sweetness of the fish dances across your tongue. With a flavor like this, there is no exaggeration—Guangfu Crispy Fish could earn a spot on *A Bite of China*!

Even the ancient city walls outside seem to nod in approval. Once a humble "rice companion" among neighbors, now a "golden clickbait" for food-content creators, this dish continues to live by the credo that "the camera eats first." No wonder netizens joke: "At Songhai Restaurant, even the fish bones are drama queens—crispy and full of flair!"

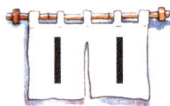

魏县魏都南大街 1555 号 · Address: No. 1555, Weidu South Street, Weixian County

吃一碗申家饸饹，品四百年人间乡愁
Eat a Bowl of Shen Family Hele and Savor Four Centuries' Homespun Longing

别小看这碗其貌不扬的面！它可是用石碾小米面与榆皮面黄金配比，用榆木饸饹床子"咔嚓"一声压出的美味奇迹！自明代起，申家十几代人坚持古法，把街头小吃熬成了省级非遗的"活化石"。

那勺祖传秘制的鲜肉卤才是灵魂所在——每天现炒的肉酱裹着榆面特有的清香，在舌尖炸开的醇厚滋味，让"赶集吃饸饹"成了刻进魏县人基因的仪式感。从田间老农到文人雅士，谁没在申家斑驳的木桌前，就着腾腾热气听过几段"饸饹演义"？这碗面里可煮着半部魏县人文史！

如今走进申家饸饹馆，老榆木工具泛着温润包浆，传承人手起床落，力道精准如旧。这早已不只是一碗面，而是一本用匠心写就的乡愁史诗，一口下去，满嘴都是四百年的光阴。

Don't underestimate this unassuming bowl of noodles. It's a culinary miracle pressed from a golden-ratio blend of stone-milled millet and elm bark flour, extruded with a satisfying *ka-cha* sound from an elm wood *hele* press! Since the Ming Dynasty, over a dozen generations of the Shen family have stuck to the ancient method, turning a humble street snack into a "living fossil" of provincial-level intangible heritage.

The soul of the dish lies in its spoonful of secret ancestral meat sauce. Freshly stir-fried daily, it coats the noodles with the unique fragrance of elm flour and bursts with savory richness. No wonder "grabbing a bowl of *hele* at the market" has become a ritual coded into the DNA of Weixian County's locals. From seasoned farmers to cultured scholars, who hasn't sat at Shen's timeworn wooden tables to listen to local lore rising with the steam?

Step into Shen's Hele Noodle Shop today, and you'll find the old elmwood tools still bearing the smooth sheen of time. The heir to the craft wields the press with practiced precision. This is far more than just a bowl of noodles. It's an epic of hometown memory written with artisan care. One bite, and you taste 400 years of history.

12

豆沫遇见"布袋"，邯郸早餐的"神仙搭档"
Meet Doumo and "Pillow Pocket," Handan's Divine Breakfast Duo

清晨的邯郸城，总被"滋溜滋溜"的声音温柔唤醒。冀南宾馆的老师傅们正用小米面打底，加入花生、芝麻、黄豆，熬制出乳黄色的"液态晨光"。而隔壁油锅里，金黄的鸡蛋"布袋"正"咕嘟咕嘟"冒着泡泡。

这对早餐界的"神仙搭档"配合得天衣无缝——先啜一口醇香的豆沫，再咬一块外酥里嫩的布袋，让米香和蛋香在口腔里跳起双人舞。红绿菜丝在豆沫里摇曳生姿，刚出锅的布袋还带着"咔嚓咔嚓"的背景音。

正如汪曾祺先生所说："四方食事，不过一碗人间烟火。"这对组合不仅承载着邯郸人三千年的早餐记忆，更用最朴实的美味诠释着：真正的经典，经得起时间的考验。

Each morning in Handan is gently awakened by the slurping sounds of *doumo* (millet- and legume-based thick porridge). In the kitchen of the Jinan Hotel, veteran chefs mix millet flour with peanuts, sesame, and soybeans to cook up a milky-golden broth—the city's liquid morning light. Meanwhile, in the fryer next door, golden egg-filled "pillow pockets" bubble and sizzle to life.

This breakfast duo is a match made in heaven: sip the rich doumo, then bite into the crispy-outside, tender-inside dough pocket—let the flavors of millet and egg twirl together in your mouth. Red and green veggie slivers sway inside the doumo, while the just-fried pocket crackles with satisfying crunch.

As author Wang Zengqi once said, "All the affairs of the world are no more than a bowl of human warmth." These two dishes carry the breakfast memories of Handan's 3,000-year story and prove, with their humble deliciousness, that true classics always stand the test of time.

冀南宾馆

13

武安市贺进镇沙洺村，S202（G234）、S312、旅游大道交汇的西南处 · Southwestern intersection of S202 (G234), S312, and Lvyou Avenue, Shaming Village, Hejin Town, Wu'an City

来一碗沙洺炒面，吃出邯郸人的江湖豪情
Have a Bowl of Shaming Stir-Fried Noodles, and Savor the Gallant Spirit of Handan

　　当夜色笼罩邯郸城，武安市沙洺村的炒面师傅们便开始了他们的"武林大会"。这碗看似普通的炒面，却藏着独门绝技——手工擀制的面条要在沸水中"修炼"至七分熟，再入铁锅与肉丝、青椒、西红柿、洋葱等"过招"。师傅手中的炒勺就是最趁手的"兵器"，翻飞间那面条就穿上了焦糖色的"战袍"。刚出锅的炒面还冒着"运功"后的热气，此刻，蒜是这道美食的"灵魂"，咬上一瓣生蒜，瞬间上头，吃起来那叫一个痛快！

　　如今，这道江湖美味，早已"开宗立派"。但老师傅们依然守着"武德"——火候要准，用料要狠，味道要稳。邯郸的饮食江湖里，沙洺炒面以其朴实无华的味道，赢得了众多食客的青睐。

　　When night falls over Handan, the stir-fried noodle masters of Shaming Village in Wu'an begin their "martial arts gathering." What appears to be an ordinary bowl of noodles conceals a signature secret technique. The hand-rolled noodles must first "train" to 70 percent doneness in boiling water, before entering the wok to spar with shredded pork, green peppers, tomatoes, onions, and other ingredients. The wok ladle in the master's hand becomes the most trusted "weapon," and as it dances, the noodles are cloaked in a caramel-colored "battle robe." Just out of the wok, the noodles still steam with inner strength;

at this moment, garlic becomes the soul of the dish. Bite into a raw clove and you'll be instantly awakened. It's a fiery and exhilarating indulgence!

Today, this bold dish of the culinary world has already established its own school of flavor. Yet the veteran chefs still uphold their "martial virtue": precise control of heat, uncompromising ingredients, and unwavering flavor. In Handan's culinary arena, Shaming stir-fried noodles have earned a devoted following with their unpretentious yet deeply satisfying taste.

14

祈五谷丰登，冀南风味背后的美好愿景
Hope for Abundant Harvests, the Beautiful Vision Behind Southern Hebei Flavors

"五谷丰登"是刻在中国人骨子里的丰收愿景。在邯郸这座三千年古城，一家以此为名的餐馆，用一桌冀南风味，演绎了土地与餐桌的深情对话。

鲍汁鱼头正在陶锅中"咕嘟"作响，鱼头胶质与鲍鱼、干贝熬成的金汤正进行着"海陆对话"；磁山砂锅鸡用文火守着千年烹调密码，揭盖时腾起的蒸汽里仿佛飘着《齐民要术》的炊香。穿花袄的服务员端上炸烹小白虾，琉璃般的脆壳下藏着白洋淀的晨露；一碟小酥肉趴在粗瓷碗里，肥瘦相间的纹理还留着案板上的刀工记忆。

十余年光阴，十三家门店，"五谷丰登"用最地道的冀南风味，让邯郸人的餐桌，成了延续农耕记忆的鲜活画卷。

Wugu Fengdeng, as a Chinese idiom which means "Abundant harvests of the five grains," is a deeply rooted aspiration in the hearts of the Chinese people. In Handan, a city with 3,000 years of history, a restaurant named after this very blessing, Wugu Fengdeng, tells a heartfelt story between land and table through a feast of southern Hebei flavors.

In a clay pot, fish head with abalone sauce simmers and bubbles, the gelatinous richness of the fish mingling with a golden broth made from abalone and dried scallops—a "dialogue between sea and land." Cishan-style chicken stew simmers over low heat, guarding age-old culinary secrets; as the lid lifts, steam rises with the fragrance of a recipe that could have been penned in *Essential Techniques for the Welfare of the People*. A server in a floral jacket brings out crispy fried white shrimp. Beneath their glassy shells lies the morning dew of Baiyangdian Lake. A plate of crispy pork bites rests in a coarse porcelain bowl, its marbled texture preserving the memory of the cleaver's craftsmanship.

Over more than a decade, with thirteen locations, Wugu Fengdeng has used the most authentic southern Hebei cuisine to turn the Handan dining table into a vibrant scroll of agrarian memory.

来一碗"面面俱到"，感受丛台迎宾馆的体贴和周到
Savor a Bowl of "Noodles with Everything Covered" to Taste Thoughtfulness at Congtai Guest House

入住丛台迎宾馆，清晨起来和邯郸人一起去公园遛个弯儿，你得瞧瞧赵武灵王亲自盖章的"战国地标"长什么样儿，顺便呼吸一下"历史的氧气"。回来肚子正好咕咕叫，绝对不能错过他家的"面面俱到"——此乃"磁州民窑"定制款，面条选用大名五得利优质面粉，采用南沿村拉面的传统工艺制作，筋道得像能拉出赵国历史那么长。四种汤底任君选，搭配十二种佐料，再来个广平无抗鸡蛋，保证让你吃出"啊，这才是古都的味道"的感叹！

当新世纪商圈的霓虹与丛台公园的月色交会时，这座方正大气的园林式建筑便成了邯郸最懂待客之道的"时空任意门"——左手CBD，右手点将台，让你在胡服骑射的豪迈与当代商务的干练中，完成一场跨越时空的角色变换。

Stay at Congtai Guest House, take a morning stroll with the locals, and witness firsthand the Warring States–period landmark personally "endorsed" by King Wuling of Zhao—then breathe in a little "oxygen from history." Just as your stomach begins to growl on the way back, don't miss their specialty: "Noodles with Everything Covered." This custom piece from the Cizhou folk kiln features premium Wudeli flour from Daming County, hand-pulled using traditional techniques from Nanyan Village, so springy they could stretch as long as Zhao State's history. Choose from four different soup bases and twelve condiments. Add a locally raised, antibiotic-free egg from Guangping County, and you'll find yourself exclaiming, "Ah—this is the taste of an ancient capital!"

When the neon lights of the New Century commercial district meet the moonlight over Congtai Park, this grand, square garden-style building transforms into a "temporal portal" that best understands the art of hospitality in Handan—CBD to your left, the General's Terrace to your right. Here, in the boldness of Wearing hufu and Practicing Mounted Archery and the efficiency of modern business life, you can effortlessly shift roles across time.

16

在丛台大酒店，尝一口让皇帝惊艳的粉皮靠肉
Savor the Emperor Jiaqing's Beloved Braised Pork with Crystal Jelly at Congtai Grand Hotel

雄踞邯郸市中心的丛台大酒店，晨光里步行三分钟即达邯郸道，暮色中推窗可见丛台的倒影，堪称串联古今的城市会客厅。

要说这里最撩动味蕾的，还得是那道粉皮靠肉。相传两百年前，一位武安老厨子带着这道菜进宫，愣是把吃惯了山珍海味的嘉庆皇帝给"鲜"着了！太行山土猪的嫩、曲周粉皮的滑，配上辽参的鲜，在咕嘟了四十八小时的高汤里"不期而遇"，碰撞出一场味觉盛宴。瞧那吸饱高汤的粉皮，晶莹剔透得像是泡了个舒坦的热水澡；土猪肉片更是嫩滑得恰到好处，指尖轻触仿佛就能沁出鲜甜的汁水来。

晨起漫步邯郸道，夜归品粉皮靠肉。这里是打开邯郸古城的钥匙，尝过皇帝惊叹的鲜美，看过丛台落日鎏金，便懂邯郸滋味原来藏在时光与美味的交错里。

Commanding Handan's heart, Congtai Grand Hotel places you steps from historic Handandao at dawn and delivers mirrored views of ancient Congtai Terrace by dusk—a timeless meeting room where past and present converge.

But the super star that dances on your palate? None other than the Braised Pork with Crystal Jelly. Legend has it that two centuries ago, a Wu'an chef brought this dish to the imperial court—and even Emperor Jiaqing, accustomed to fancy delicacies, was stunned by its freshness! Tender Taihang mountain pork, silky Quzhou starch jelly, and briny Liaodong sea cucumber converge in a 48-hour simmered broth, orchestrating a symphony of textures. Watch how the jelly, now translucent after soaking up the rich stock, glisten like jewels fresh from a spa; while the pork slices yield at the slightest touch, threatening to release their sweet, savory nectar.

Begin your morning strolling Handandao, and end your night savoring imperial-approved Braised Pork with Crystal Jelly—this is the key to touching the city's soul. Taste the dish that conquered the tastebud of the throne, watch twilight gild Congtai's stones, and you'll grasp Handan's secret: time itself simmers in every sublime bite.

17

肥乡区丛台酒业将相和大道 (309 国道旁) · Jiangxianghe Avenue,
Congtai Liquor Industry, Feixiang District (beside National Highway 309)

置酒丛台上，醉此际会，风云自来
Come to Congtai Winery, Getting Drunk at This Gathering, and Letting Destiny Unfold Itself

外乡人初至邯郸，总先被一缕酒香牵住。唐代岑参曾叹"伤心丛台下，一旦生蔓草"。诗人独酌丛台，寥寥数语，道尽荒芜寂寥。今观丛台，已非昔日蔓草荒台，唯有丛台酒的醇香依旧氤氲——这缕醇香，承载着"鲁酒薄而邯郸围"的历史典故，延续着光武帝"丛台置酒"的雄才大略，更凝结着"贞元增烧坊"五百年的匠心传承。

你若循着诗踪而来，丛台酒苑将以千年陈酿相迎。孟德"对酒当歌，人生几何"之感慨，太白"醉骑白花马，西走邯郸城"之疏狂，梅村"丛台置酒风萧索"之悲凉——千载风云际会，尽付杯中沉浮。这杯"河北第一名酒"，当得起"南有茅台，北有丛台"的美誉。

如今的丛台酒苑，已从老酒坊发展为集酿酒、科研、旅游于一体的4A级景区，延续酿造古法，更铸就新篇。来丛台酒苑，共饮此杯千年风华。

Handan greets tourists with a fragrance of wine. The Tang poet Cen Shen once sighed beneath Congtai, "My heart breaks to see wild vines claim Congtai." His solitary verses painted Congtai's desolation. Today, Congtai stands no longer in ruins, yet the mellow aroma of Congtai Wine still lingers—this very essence carries a tale of "the thin wine of the Lu State caused Handan's siege," echoes Emperor Guangwu's strategic toasts upon the height, and condenses five centuries' inheritance of craft from Zhenyuanzeng Distillery.

Follow the trail of poetry to Congtai Winery, where millennia-aged brews await your homage. Here, Cao Cao's "Sing with wine, for life is fleeting" lingers in the air; Li Bai's "In drunkenness, I ride a white-flowered steed, heading west to Handan" still echoes; Wu Weiye's (1609–1672) lament of "desolate winds over Congtai's cups" still whispers. A millennium of triumphs and sorrows distilled into every drop. Acclaimed as "Hebei's finest wine," it truly lives up to its high status—where "Moutai reigns south, Congtai dominates north."

Today's Congtai Winery has evolved from an ancient cellar into a 4A-rated scenic area blending traditional brewing, scientific innovation, and cultural tourism, where modern techniques continue aged mastery. Let's toast—this vintage carries a millennium of legend, yet tastes eternally new.

　　当百里青峦学会呼吸，雾纱是它黎明的哈气，苔阶收集昨夜星露，松风在树隙间流转成液态绿意。慢些走——山正煮茶，水在调弦，每一处转角，邯郸的温柔总是欲说还休，等风来读。

　　When the endless peaks learn to breathe, the morning mist becomes their dawn exhalation. Moss-covered steps gather last night's stardew, while pine breezes flow through trees like liquid jade. Pace slowly—the mountains are steeping tea, the streams are tuning their strings, and at every turn, Handan's tenderness lingers—unspoken, waiting for the wind to unfold.

百里青峦
见悠然

Where Endless Peaks Cradle Unhurried Joy

01

登太行五指山，触摸天地掌纹
Ascend Wuzhi Mountain and Touch the Palm Lines of Heaven and Earth

　　五指山位于涉县的太行山东麓，相传孙悟空被如来佛封印于此参禅悟道。这里主峰海拔一千二百八十三米，整座山如同大自然挥洒的绿绸缎，以"雄奇险秀"惊艳四方。最神奇的是，连绵三公里的山体竟天然勾勒出一尊仰天卧佛：自东向西，发髻、鼻峰、喉结轮廓分明，双脚趾直指苍穹。大佛静卧于太行之巅，仿佛在云端小憩，又似在静听千年松涛。登顶高山草甸，听山风、看流云、赏瀑布，脚下是华北罕见的柔软绿毯或金黄绒被，眼前是卧佛奇观，随手一拍就是大片！

　　冒险爱好者可挑战一百八十八米高的3D玻璃桥、落差八十九米的峡谷漂流，还有永不落幕的西游"真人秀"正在"悟空谷"上演，钻水帘洞、和真人"猴哥"合影，让童年回忆杀在此拉满。

Wuzhi Mountain lies on the eastern slopes of the Taihang Mountains in Shexian County. According to legend, it was here that the Monkey King, Sun Wukong, was sealed beneath the mountain by the Buddha to meditate and seek enlightenment. The main peak rises to an elevation of 1,283 meters, and the entire mountain unfurls like a verdant silk ribbon cast by nature itself. Wuzhi Mountain stuns visitors with its fourfold beauty—majestic, steep, picturesque, and graceful. Its most astonishing feature is a naturally formed, 3-kilometer-long silhouette of a reclining Buddha. Facing the sky from east to west, the contours of his topknot, nose, Adam's apple, and toes are all vividly distinguishable, and his feet point straight toward the heavens. The great Buddha rests atop the Taihang peaks, as if napping among the clouds or quietly listening to the millennia-old murmurs of the pine forests. At the summit's alpine meadows, the mountain wind hums through, clouds drift by, and waterfalls cascade down the cliffs. Beneath your feet stretches a rare blanket of soft green, or golden, depending on the season, while before you lies the awe-inspiring sight of the reclining Buddha. Every photo is a masterpiece.

For thrill-seekers, there's an 188-meter-tall 3D glass bridge and an 89-meter drop canyon rafting course through a steep gorge. And in "Wukong Valley," a live-action Journey to the West experience is always on. Step into the Water Curtain Cave and take a selfie with a real-life "Monkey King"—a nostalgic journey back to your childhood.

02

到大洼村，看看太行山里的"石头乐高"
Visit Dawa Village Where Taihang Mountains Hide "Stone Lego" Wonders

欢迎来到现实版"我的世界"——大洼村，这里的村民都是隐藏的乐高大师！明朝嘉靖年间，张姓家族躲进太行山，用石头搭出二十八代人的"魔幻城堡"。云雾缭绕时，层层叠叠的石头四合院在云端若隐若现，被称作太行山里的"布达拉宫"。这里的石头会"套娃"：院叠院、房赶房，独拱石桥全靠力学奇迹。村民过着佛系生活——毛驴当快递小哥，山柴炖菜香飘十里，石磨碾着比咖啡机还慢的岁月。最绝的是那座网红石拱桥，白天是力学教科书，晚上秒变鹊桥会，五百年来见证的爱情故事比偶像剧还甜。

Welcome to the real-life version of Minecraft—Dawa Village, where locals are secretly master Lego builders! During the Jiajing reign of the Ming Dynasty (1522–1566), the Zhang family retreated into the Taihang Mountains and constructed a "magical fortress" of stone, passed down through 28 generations. When mist shrouds the peaks, the stacked stone courtyards appear and vanish like a dream in the clouds, earning it the nickname "Potala Palace of the Taihang Mountains." Here, stone structures are nested like matryoshka dolls: courtyard within courtyard, room adjoining room. Its signature single-arch stone bridges are held together entirely through the miracles of mechanics. Life in the village flows at a relaxed pace: donkeys serve as deliverymen, stews made with mountain firewood waft their fragrance for miles, and time grinds slowly in stone mills, even slower than a coffee machine. The star attraction? A viral stone arch bridge—a structural engineering case study by day and a bridge of love under the stars by night—has witnessed romances sweeter than any TV drama over the past 500 years.

03

游朝阳沟，唱一曲永不落幕的山乡恋歌
Explore Chaoyanggou Gully and Sing an Enduring Love Song of the Mountains

锣鼓点一响，山风自带伴奏——欢迎来到豫剧顶流、国民结婚曲《朝阳沟》的故事原生地！藏在武安管陶乡的这片青山绿水，不仅是银环与栓保上演知识青年下乡记的舞台，更是一处世外桃源。

沿着当年银环进山的石板路拾级而上，老房东拴保娘家的土坯房还在原地候场。转角遇见写着"朝阳沟"三字的巨石，瞬间激活脑海中的豫剧旋律——"咱两个在学校整整三年"！

到山涧旁吼一嗓子"亲家母你坐下"，回声就是最捧场的票友；在田间地头寻访剧中场景，分分钟解锁"主角同款"打卡照。当夕阳把山峦染成金幕布，晚风送来板胡的悠扬，坐在农家小院啃一口甜掉牙的柿子，你会顿悟：山里人家的烟火生活，早已酿成比戏词更绵长的回甘。

As the drums begin to beat, the mountain breeze provides the perfect accompaniment—welcome to the birthplace of *Chaoyanggou*, the beloved Yu opera hit and wedding anthem of a generation! Nestled in the lush landscapes of Guantao Township in Wu'an, this hidden gem was not only the stage where Yinhuan and Shuanbao's tale of educated youth returning to the countryside first unfolded, but also a genuine Arcadia beyond the mundane world.

Climb the same flagstone path Yinhuan once walked into the hills, and you'll find the original adobe home of Shuanbao's family still patiently waiting in its place. Turn a corner and you'll see a giant boulder engraved with the words "Chaoyanggou," instantly evoking that unforgettable melody in one of Yu operas: "We've been together at school for three full years…"

Belt out "Dear mother-in-law, please have a seat," another line of lyrics, by the mountain stream and let the echo be your most enthusiastic fan. Stroll the fields in search of scenes from the opera and strike a pose to match the main characters. As the sun sets and paints the mountains gold, the gentle strains of the *banhu* (a traditional instrument) drift in on the breeze. Sitting in a farmhouse courtyard, biting into a honey-sweet persimmon, you'll understand—the everyday life of mountain folks has brewed a richness that lingers longer than any lyric.

涉县井店镇·Jingdian Town, Shexian County

来王金庄，看石头变梯田
Visit Wangjinzhuang Village and Witness How Stone Becomes Terraces

走进王金庄村，准备好被漫山遍野的"石头魔法"震撼吧！这里有联合国认证的"全球重要农业文化遗产"——涉县旱作石堰梯田！想象一下，祖辈们在太行山的石头沟壑里，硬是靠双手垒起层层叠叠、蜿蜒如龙的石堰梯田。

石屋、石街、石磨、石桥，村子本身就是座活着的"石头博物馆"，处处散发着古朴沧桑的味道。梯田里藏着农业智慧：花椒树扎根田边固土留水，梯田间谷子、玉米昂首挺立，绿豆、红小豆匍匐其间，眉豆沿石堰攀缘而上——五彩斑斓的抗旱混种法加之水窖存雨的本事，让梯田在少雨之地依然生机勃发。来王金庄，看石头如何变良田，感受在石缝里种满希望的传奇，学习农民对抗天地的生存智慧与吃苦耐劳的奋斗精神！

Step into Wangjinzhuang Village and prepare to be awed by a landscape sculpted in stone. This is home to the Shexian County Dryland Stone Terraced System, a site recognized by the United Nations as a "Globally Important Agricultural Heritage System." Imagine generations of ancestors using nothing but their hands to construct layer upon layer of stone terraces that coil across the rugged Taihang terrain like dragons.

Stone houses, stone streets, stone mills, and stone bridges—the village itself is a living "stone museum," steeped in ancient rustic charm. Wisdom lies hidden in the fields: Sichuan pepper trees planted at terrace edges help retain water and prevent erosion; millet and corn stand tall between the terraces, while mung beans and red adzuki beans crawl along the ground, and rice beans climb up the stone walls. This vivid drought-resistant intercropping system, combined with rainwater harvesting in cisterns, keeps the terraces bursting with life even in arid conditions. Come to Wangjinzhuang and see how stone transforms into fertile field—a miracle sown in the cracks of rock. Let's learn from the farmers' endurance, resilience, and deep-rooted wisdom in facing nature's challenges.

05

去七步沟，把太行山的"呼吸"装进肺里
Hike at Qibu Valley Where the Taihang Mountains Breathe

七步沟风景

武安的七步沟，原名"漆铺沟"。唐朝时，僧侣们被这里的满山漆树和清幽环境吸引，跑来隐居修行，用佛家"七步莲花"典故给它改了名。清朝文人在《罗汉洞碑记》里疯狂呐喊："此何境也？非天也，非地也，非人间也！"

如今这片山水宝藏，集齐了六大主题副本——汉风山门刻着欧阳中石题字；百瀑峡甩开两公里水袖，雨季时瀑布喷洒的水雾凉透整个夏天；天镜湖则像被群山捧起的翡翠，二十米深的深潭美到犯规；更有东汉马武寨练兵场和八路军一二九师医院遗址，见证从古至今的变迁！

"七步莲花开，仙沟引客来。"春揽山花，夏扑飞瀑，秋醉红叶，冬冲滑雪，来七步沟，发现属于你的四季惊喜。

Qibu Valley (literally means "Seven-Step Valley") in Wu'an, formerly known as Qipu Valley, got its present name during the Tang Dynasty. Monks, enchanted by the fragrant lacquer trees and the serene surroundings, chose it as a site for reclusion and named it after the Buddhist story of the "Seven Steps to Lotus Blossoms," where lotuses bloomed at each step of the newborn Buddha. In the *Inscription of Arhat Cave*, a Qing Dynasty scholar exclaimed, "What realm is this? Neither heaven, nor earth, nor the mortal world!"

Today, this treasure trove of nature offers six themed areas: A Han-style mountain gate carved with calligraphy by Ouyang Zhongshi; Baibu Gorge unfurling its two-kilometer-long sleeves of waterfalls—during the rainy season, the mists cool the whole summer; Tianjing Lake, a jade basin embraced by the mountains, boasts a mesmerizing 20-meter-deep pool; and historical sites like the Eastern Han (25–220) Mawuzhai drill ground and the former hospital of the 129th Division of the Eighth Route Army trace the area's long arc of change.

"Seven steps and lotus blossoms bloom; the fairy valley draws visitors soon." In spring, take in mountain blossoms; in summer, chase waterfalls; in autumn, revel in crimson leaves; in winter, dash down snowy slopes. At Qibu Valley, each season offers its own surprise.

06

探龙洞珠泉，解锁山腹里的"水晶盲盒"
Venture into Dragon Cave and Pearl Spring Where a Crystal "Blind Box" Hides in the Mountain's Heart

在邯郸市峰峰矿区的滏阳河源头，藏着一处"龙洞珠泉"奇观！这里神麇山与南鼓山南北对峙，传说幽深的黑龙洞中潜藏着掌控风雨的黑龙，古人曾惊叹"骊龙出洞去，洞深不可测"。《水经注》记载它"泉源奋涌，滚滚如汤"。泉水自幽深洞穴汩汩涌出，水花在光影里旋舞成珠。

洞顶有始建于唐代的黑龙庙，飞檐斗拱的风月关石券上刻着"风月关"三字，登阁可见明代进士的诗碑，古韵十足。如今这里变身活力水乐园！沿滏阳河漫步，你能踩过清浊分界的"珠链栈道"，在天然泉水泳池挑战冬泳，或扫码接一杯甘甜直饮水……快来打卡，一起探索这处自然造就的"骊龙秘境"吧！

At the source of the Fuyang River in Handan's Fengfeng Mining District lies the spectacular "Dragon Cave and Pearl Spring." Nestled between Shenmi Mountain to the north and Nangu Mountain to the south, this site is steeped in legend. Deep within the shadowy Black Dragon Cave is said to dwell a dragon that commands the wind and rain. Ancient texts marveled, "The black dragon emerges, the cave unfathomable." According to the *Commentary on the Water Classic*, its waters "surge forth, boiling like soup." Springs gush from the depths of the cave, water droplets sparkling like pearls as they dance through light and shadow.

Atop the cave sits the Black Dragon Temple, originally built in the Tang Dynasty. On the stone archway of Fengyue Pass, flying eaves and bracket sets still frame the inscribed characters "Fengyue Pass." Climb the tower to find steles inscribed with verses by Ming Dynasty scholars—timeless poetry etched in stone. Today, the area has been transformed into a lively aquatic playground. Strolling along the Fuyang River, you can find the "pearl chain plank path" that divides clear and turbid waters, a natural spring pool daring you to try winter swimming, or a sip of sweet, drinkable spring water by scanning a QR code. Come and unlock this hidden "Black Dragon Realm," crafted by the hand of nature!

07

览东太行，触摸云端的丹霞秘境
Tour Eastern Taihang Where a Danxia Wonderland Lies Among the Clouds

　　巍巍太行之东，藏着大地最炽热的告白。乘索道穿云而上，脚下是刀削斧劈的绝壁，身旁是翻涌的雾海，忽然一阵风吹过，云海散开，万亩松林在山坳里铺成绿毯，红岩栈道如赤色丝带缠绕峰峦，最险处仅容一人侧身而过，低头可见深渊万丈，抬头便是澄碧苍穹。还有勇敢者的游戏——飞拉达，扣紧钢索攀过岩壁，看脚下云海翻涌，指尖攀着的不只是岩点，更是把太行踩在脚下的豪情。

　　行至最高海拔一千四百二十八米处，伸手仿佛能摘到流云。若遇雨后初晴，整座山便成了天然画布，彩虹架在红岩与绿林之间，栈道上的水汽折射出七彩光晕，恍若踏霞而行。

　　待到暮色浸染山巅，夕阳为红岩镀上金箔，山风送来松涛阵阵，此刻静坐观景台，看云海沉为墨色，星星缀满天鹅绒般的夜空——享受"偷得浮生半日，闲看云卷云舒，尽享人间清欢"的浪漫氛围。

To the east of the grand Taihang range lies the land's most passionate confession. Ascend by cable car, soaring through the clouds. Below you, cliffs are sheared and chiseled like works of art; around you, a sea of fog billows and rolls. Suddenly, a breeze clears the mist, revealing a vast pine forest carpeting the valleys like green velvet. A red rock plank path winds through the peaks like a crimson ribbon. At its narrowest, it allows only one person to pass sideways—look down, and you see a chasm without end; look up, and there's the brilliant blue sky. Adrenaline seekers can tackle the via ferrata, a vertical climbing route where hands grip metal cables across sheer rock. Below, clouds churn; above, your fingers grasp more than just the rock—you hold the exhilaration of conquering Taihang itself.

At the summit, 1,428 meters high, you can almost pluck clouds from the sky. After rain, the mountain becomes a natural canvas—rainbows arch between red cliffs and green woods, while mist on the plank path refracts into seven-colored halos. It's as if you're walking on light.

When dusk cloaks the mountaintop, the sunset gilds the red cliffs with gold, and the wind carries the sound of rustling pines. Sitting quietly on a viewing platform, you'll watch the sea of clouds darken like ink and stars pin the velvet sky. Here, in stolen hours of serenity, find life's poetry: where clouds dance, and the soul breathes.

08

闯赤水湾，解锁古镇全息剧本杀
Unlock a Holographic Scripted Experience in Chishuiwan Ancient Town

赤水湾古镇，依偎在漳河的臂弯里，石桥、木桥勾连起婉转街巷，白墙灰瓦，乌篷船摇橹而过。白天能到工坊街推石磨点卤水做豆腐、踩织布机感受经纬穿梭，还能啃一口麦香炸裂的老酵子馒头；夜幕降临后，55.9 米高的"华北第一塔"文昌塔化身光影魔术师，《风华涉县》实景大秀点亮山野。

如果想一探成语背后的故事，那不妨去一趟成语老街，"补天浴日""一字不易""登楼望阙"主题布景将邯郸成语典故玩成活态剧本杀。聚星堂天天上演《李府招亲》的互动好戏，还有崇州县衙、状元府、文峰书院，花式打卡古代职场与科举人生。这座活力四射的小镇，正以最潮的方式展现满满的太行风情。

Nestled in the crook of the Zhanghe River, Chishuiwan Ancient Town weaves together winding alleyways with stone and wooden bridges. Whitewashed walls and gray-tiled roofs line the way as black-awning boats glide gently by. By day, head to Workshop Street to grind tofu with a stone mill and press brine into curds, or feel the shuttle fly on a traditional loom. Sink your teeth into an old-style sourdough steamed bun bursting with the fragrance of wheat. When night falls, the 55.9-meter-tall Wenchang Tower, known as the "tallest tower in North China," transforms into a master of light and shadow. The open-air performance *Elegance of She County* lights up the surrounding mountains.

Curious about the stories behind Chinese idioms? Stroll down the Idiom Old Street, where immersive sets themed around classics like "Patching the Sky and Bathing in the Sun," "A Single Word Not to Be

Changed," and "Climbing the Tower to Gaze Toward the Capital" turn idiomatic lore into a live-action script game. At Juxing Hall, the interactive drama *The Li Family Seeks a Son-in-Law* plays daily. Explore the County Magistrate Office of Chongzhou, the Mansion of the Top Scholar, and the Wenfeng Academy to check in at ancient career venues and step into the highs and lows of the imperial examination system. This dynamic town showcases Taihang culture in the trendiest of ways.

09

溯太行花溪谷，527块古磨盘邀你来转
Walk the Taihang Huaxi Valley Maze Where 527 Ancient Millstones Await Your Turn

在河北邯郸武安太行花溪谷，藏着一座"世界唯一"的水上奇观——九曲黄河阵！它用527块明清古磨盘搭建而成（每块重达150公斤），像一座漂浮在水面的神秘迷宫。

这里原是古代兵家"易守难攻"的战场，因形似黄河九曲十八弯得名，如今成了祈福圣地——民间流传"转转九曲阵，百病消、万事顺"，走一圈就能讨个好彩头！

除了奇阵，花溪谷本身也是宝藏！景区绿荫蔽日，溪湖瀑布串联成链，蝶瓣湖、驼峰岭美如水墨画，负氧离子含量极高，可谓休闲养生好去处。进山路铺满磨盘像"铜钱大道"，山顶还有浪漫的"三生石"，情侣打卡必喊："相约花溪谷，缘定三生石"！快带上好奇心和相机，解锁这步步惊喜的"迷途浪漫"吧！

In the Huaxi Valley of Wu'an, Handan, Hebei lies a one-of-a-kind marvel—the Nine-Bend Yellow River Formation, the world's only floating water maze made entirely of millstones! Comprising 527 millstones from the Ming and Qing dynasties, each weighing 150 kilograms, the labyrinth floats atop the water like a mysterious spellbinding pattern.

Originally designed as a battlefield known for its strategic defense, it resembles the meandering Yellow River, hence the name. Today, it has become a sacred site for blessings. Locals believe: "Walk the Nine-Bend Maze, and illnesses vanish, good fortune follows." One trip through the maze may just bring you luck!

But the maze is only the beginning. Huaxi Valley is a hidden treasure in itself. Its shaded landscapes feature interconnected streams, lakes, and waterfalls. Places like Butterfly Petal Lake and Camel Ridge are as beautiful as ink paintings. With its high concentration of negative oxygen ions, it's truly an ideal retreat for relaxation and wellness. The entrance road is paved with millstones like a "Path of Coins." At the mountain's summit awaits the romantic "Three Lives Stone," where couples exclaim, "Meet at Huaxi Valley, love sealed for three lifetimes!" Pack your curiosity and camera—every turn here is a romantic twist in this enchanting "maze of wonder."

愿始终绿意呀 站在瀑布下的应该是两个人
我在花溪谷等你
西   花笼潭   东

我爱你 ♡

♡ I LOVE YOU

10

闯韩王九寨，看奇峰揽胜，品汉韵千年
Conquer the Nine Villages of Han King Where Scenic Peaks Meet Epic Legends of Han Dynasty

想一秒穿越千年，邂逅韩信点兵的豪情？来韩王九寨就对了！传说汉将韩信曾在此屯兵点将，连山峰都自带"王者光环"！

想打卡神仙同款？那就在黎明冲顶揽胜阁，看红日喷薄、云海鎏金。最绝的是"韩山戴雨"奇观——山下晴空万里，山顶云雾裹雨，分分钟上演仙侠剧！韩王谷更绝——点将台喊一嗓子，饮马涧遛个弯，再闯汉军史馆摸青铜剑。下山前别错过红河谷的巨型稻田画，四种彩稻拼出大地艺术。而那条串起红河谷火车乐园、狐仙月季园的百里天路，直通玻璃悬空观日台，脚下云海翻滚，随手一拍都是神仙朋友圈！免费入园的快乐，赶紧冲！

Want to be transported through time in a single breath—to meet the spirit of General Han Xin (?–196 BC) commanding troops? Hanwang Jiuzhai (literally means the "Nine Villages of Han King") is your destination! Legend has it that Han Xin once encamped here, and even the peaks still carry an aura of command.

Hoping for a view fit for the immortals? Climb at dawn to Lansheng Pavilion for a panoramic sunrise and golden sea of clouds. The most breathtaking scene is the rare phenomenon "Han Mountain Wearing Rain"—where sunny skies reign below while the summit is shrouded in misty rain, like a fantasy world brought to

life! Han King Valley offers even more: shout from the Commanding Platform, stroll through the Horse Water Ravine, and stop by the Han Army History Museum to touch authentic bronze swords. Before heading down the mountain, don't miss the enormous rice paddy artwork in Red River Valley. Four varieties of colored rice come together in a living landscape painting. A hundred-mile scenic route connects Red River Valley's train-themed amusement park and Fox Fairy Rose Garden, leading all the way to a glass-floored skywalk where waves of clouds roll beneath your feet. Every photo is straight out of a celestial postcard. And yes—it's free to enter, so bookmark it and go!

游京娘湖，见证一湖山水里的千年"狗粮"
Cruise Jingniang Lake Where a Timeless Romance Ripples in Every Wave

　　前方高甜水域，请备好"柠檬"入场！京娘湖这汪被太行山捧在手心的碧水，可是宋太祖赵匡胤给京娘写的"千年情书"。相传赵匡胤曾英雄救美，千里护送姑娘京娘回家，途中险象环生却不离不弃，后人便将这片山水命名为"京娘湖"。

　　乘船游湖必打卡"倒人字"形水道，在东支仙灵峡可看鹊桥、屏风山如画卷展开，到西支京娘峡可寻梳妆台、搭衣岩。下船后玩法更嗨：登贞义岛探京娘祠，乘缆车直上云中寺俯瞰全景；胆大的可以走高空玻璃栈道，感受心跳加速，或坐四千米长的山地过山车穿梭林间，再挑战高空速滑让湖光山色扑面而来。玩累了？武安拽面、烩菜、驴肉配活水醋，酸香开胃；夜宿山间民宿，枕星河入梦，晨起看云雾绕峰，这才叫神仙日子！

Warning:high-sweetness waters ahead—lemons optional! Cradled in the palms of the Taihang Mountains, Jingniang Lake is a shimmering love letter penned by Zhao Kuangyin, Emperor Taizu of Song, to a woman named Jingniang. Legend has it Zhao Kuangyin heroically rescued Jingniang and escorted her across vast distances to her home, braving countless dangers without leaving her side. This moving tale of devotion led to the naming of this serene landscape—Jingniang Lake.

Must-see spots during the boat ride include the inverted V-shaped waterway. Magpie Bridge and the Screen Mountain unfold like a living scroll in the East Xianling Gorge. In the West Jingniang Gorge, Dressing Table Rock and Clothes-Hanging Cliff await. Off the boat, the excitement continues: explore Zhenyi Island and the Jingniang Temple, take a cable car to the Yunzhong Temple for a bird's-eye views. Daredevils can test their nerves on the glass skywalk, zoom through forests on a 4km mountain coaster, or launch into lakeside zip-lining with scenery rushing at you. Hungry now? Dig into Wu'an-style hand-pulled noodles, stew, and donkey meat with fresh vinegar—tangy and refreshing. At night, stay in a mountain homestay, fall asleep under the stars, and wake to clouds twining around the peaks. Now that's the immortal lifestyle!

12

访古武当，翻张三丰的修仙备忘录！
Visit Ancient Wudang and Flip Through Zhang Sanfeng's Taoist Playbook

古武当山从太行云海中探出头来，赤壁丹崖是它披了千年的赭红道袍。相传张三丰曾在此悟道，它可是比南方武当更早的"道教祖庭"，唐代古碑上"古武当山"的记载让它名震四方。

真武大帝与张三丰的千年古庙矗立在极顶。北顶老爷顶和南顶奶奶顶由惊险天桥相连，走一趟魂儿都飘到仙境里！山中奇石更是鬼斧神工："大鹏展翅"欲冲天，"神猴献瑞"捧仙桃，"毛公峰"侧影如伟人，"鲁迅峰"沉思望山河，还有巨型"太极掌"暗合阴阳玄机。

乘缆车直上金顶，滑千米速溜下山，再挑战高空秋千与飞仙滑索，尖叫体验拉满！朝圣、避暑、寻奇、玩心跳——这座太行秘境的仙气与野趣，等你来解锁！

Peeking through the cloud seas of the Taihang Mountains, Ancient Wudang Mountain wears its red cliffs like a Taoist robe draped for over a thousand years. It is said that Taoist master Zhang Sanfeng attained enlightenment here, making it an even older Taoist sanctuary than its southern namesake. Inscriptions on a Tang Dynasty stele bearing the name "Ancient Wudang Mountain" have brought it wide acclaim.

At its summit stands the ancient temple of the Great True Warrior Emperor, major Taoist deity, and Zhang Sanfeng, still serene after a thousand years. The northern Laoye Peak and southern Nainai Peak are joined by a dizzying sky bridge, a path so surreal it feels like walking in a dream. The mountain's rocks are nature's masterpieces: "Great Roc Spreads Wings" poised for flight, "Divine Monkey Offering Peach" with a sacred fruit in hand, "Chairman Mao Peak" with its side profile reminiscent of the great leader, and "Lu Xun Peak" lost in thought gazing over the land. There's even a massive "Tai Chi Palm" echoing the mysteries of yin and yang.

Take a cable car to the Golden Summit, then slide down a thousand-meter slope, or try the high-altitude swing and flying zipline—each thrilling enough to make you scream with joy. Whether for pilgrimage, summer retreat, natural wonders, or an adrenaline rush, this hidden gem of the Taihang Mountains is ready to reveal its divine charm and wild delight.

13

在漫宁民宿，枕山眠云，邂逅慢时光
Retreat to Manning Homestay Where Mountains Pillow Your Dreams and Clouds Tuck You In

在太行山海拔九百米处的云海里，漫宁民宿正用古院落收藏着都市人遗失的慢时光。四十三间客房像被山风吻过的调色盘，各具主题——温馨可爱的公主房、硬核前卫的太空房、温馨缱绻的家庭房，总有一款能接住您疲惫的身心。

清晨，汤池里的山泉水映着朝霞；午后，陶艺转盘上的泥土还带着阳光的温度。智能语音系统也懂得适时沉默，留白给山风与鸟鸣的对谈。夜色渐浓时，浴室的香氛悄然舒展，吹风机的暖风轻抚发丝，连现代科技都放低了声响，生怕惊扰了山居的静谧。

漫宁民宿懂得，真正的奢侈，是把时光过成诗。在这里，连发呆都是一种修行，每一次呼吸都是与自然的对话。

At 900 meters above sea level, in the cloud-kissed heights of the Taihang Mountains, Manning Homestay preserves the slow life urban dwellers have long forgotten within its restored ancient courtyard. Its 43 guest rooms are a palette painted by mountain breezes, each with a unique theme. From cozy princess chambers to edgy space-themed rooms and warm family suites—every room here is a haven for your tired soul.

In the morning, mountain spring water in the hot tub reflects the glow of dawn. In the afternoon, the clay on the pottery wheel holds the lingering warmth of sunlight. Even the voice-activated smart system knows when to be silent—leaving space for the mountain breeze to converse with birdsong. As night falls, the fragrance in the bathroom subtly unfurls. A warm dryer breeze caresses your hair. Even modern technology lowers its voice, not to disturb the tranquility of mountain life.

Manning Homestay understands: true luxury is turning time into poetry. Here, even spacing out becomes a form of meditation, and each breath a dialogue with nature.

武安市活水乡东太行景区游客中心旁 · Next to the East Taihang
Scenic Area Visitor Center, Huoshui Township, Wu'an City

去晨曦酒店，睡在山水画里，醒在云端上
Stay at Chenxi Hotel to Dream in a Landscape Painting and Wake Above the Clouds

谁说景区酒店都是千篇一律？东太行晨曦酒店偏偏不走寻常路——新中式的雅致里藏着几分俏皮，从亲子套房的童话世界到湖景套房，"承包整片山水"，总有一款能让您赖床的理由升级。

想体验隐士生活？石八酒民宿的八个院落将陶渊明的理想照进现实；想犒赏味蕾？四个特色餐厅正用太行山珍演绎"舌尖上的风雅颂"。无柱宴会厅可容下星辰大海，无边泳池则把云霞酿成鸡尾酒。

这里最懂现代人的"两栖"哲学：健身房里的自律与床头《庄子》的逍遥游在此和解——毕竟望着太行云海发呆，本就是最高级的禅修。晨曦酒店像个会读心的老友，知道您想要的不只是一夜好眠，更是一段可收藏的山水光阴。

Who says scenic hotels are all the same? Chenxi Hotel in East Taihang dares to be different. Amidst the elegance of new Chinese style, it hides a playful heart. From whimsical parent-child suites to lakeside rooms with private views of mountains and waters, each stay gives you a new reason to linger in bed.

Seeking a recluse's retreat? The eight courtyards of Shibajiu Homestay turn Tao Yuanming's pastoral dreams into reality. Want to treat your palate? Four specialty restaurants reinterpret Taihang's mountain delicacies into a banquet of elegance. The pillarless banquet hall can hold stars and dreams, and the infinity pool turns sunset clouds into cocktails.

This place understands the "amphibious" life of modern people, balancing gym discipline with the free-spirited musings of *Zhuangzi* by the bedside. After all, gazing at cloud seas while lost in thought is the ultimate form of Zen. Like an old friend who reads your heart, Chenxi Hotel knows you seek more than sleep—but a keepsake of time that mountains and waters linger in your memories forever.

15

穿行于三百里天路的百里画廊，每一次转弯都是相逢

Wind Through the Hundred-Mile Gallery Road, Every Turn Bringing a New Encounter

当五条公路在太行山腹地挥毫泼墨，便绘就了这幅三百里长的立体山水——旅游大道串起红色记忆与田园诗篇，武当大道在崇山峻岭间架起天路，平安大道将八大景区拥入怀中，盘龙大道诉说古今传奇，白云大道则连接起晋冀两省的烟火人间。

摇下车窗，山风会送来采摘园的果香；停下脚步，驿站里的咖啡正冒着热气。骑行道的勇士们早已汗流浃背，而自驾客们还在等待被下一个转弯处的风景惊艳。这些公路最懂"欲速则不达"的哲理——在这里，八十码是激情，六十码是享受，三十码才是读懂太行的正确速度。想体验刺激的，来"机车旅游文化节"，在机车赛道释放全部激情！当车窗框住云海时，你会恍然大悟：原来太行山最美的风景，从来不在终点，而在每个转弯后的那个瞬间。

When five roads streak across the heart of the Taihang Mountains, they paint a three-dimensional scroll 300 *li* (about 150 kilometers) long. The Travel Avenue strings together red history and pastoral idylls. Wudang Avenue forges a skyway through lofty peaks. Ping'an Avenue cradles eight scenic zones.

Panlong Avenue tells tales of ancient and modern legends. Baiyun Avenue connects daily life across Shanxi and Hebei.

Roll down your windows, and the mountain breeze will carry the scent of fruit from nearby orchards. Pause for a break, and steaming coffee awaits at the roadside inn. Cyclists sweat it out on the lanes, while drivers gasp at the next scenic turn. These roads know the truth behind "More haste, less speed." Here, 80 kilometers per hour is passion and 60 is enjoyment. But 30—that's when you truly understand Taihang. When your car window frames a sea of clouds, you'll realize: the most beautiful view of the Taihang Mountains is never at the end—it's in the magic that unfolds after every turn.

想知道邯郸是怎么让传统文化在新时代焕发光彩的吗？这里有十七个超有料的新空间，就像一场传统与现代的精彩对话！跟着它们逛一圈，你会发现邯郸悄悄把历史记忆、公共空间、产业升级和艺术再生这四个维度拧成一股绳，造出了一套超赞的城市生活新玩法。

Curious how Handan breathes new life into traditional culture in the modern era? Here you'll find seventeen dynamic new spaces, each one a vivid dialogue between heritage and innovation! As you stroll through them, you'll see how Handan subtly weaves together history, public space, industrial upgrading, and artistic regeneration into one cohesive thread, creating a bold, new way to experience urban life.

千年古城变形记

The Metamorphosis of a Millennia-Old City

01

丛台区光明大街与丛台路交叉口南行 100 米路西 · 100 meters south of the intersection of Guangming Street and Congtai Road, west side of the road, Hanbaofang, Congtai District

打卡邯宝坊，拆一个装满"邯郸灵感"的盲盒
Check in at Hanbaofang to Unwrap a Blind Box Full of Handan-Inspired Surprises

"别人卖纪念品，我卖城市烟火气！"邯宝坊一开门就自带傲娇气场——二十个区县在此"神仙打架"，线上线下齐发力，把最地道的农产、文创、文旅好物一网打尽。

古老与现代的气息在此交融：磁州窑的古雅线条，溜上了温润茶具；回车巷里蔺相如的谦让故事，印成了潮酷卫衣上的标语；那些源自邯郸、流传千年的成语智慧，则被设计师点化成憨态可掬、寓意深长的玩偶与文具。

无论是寻找一份独特的城市记忆，还是为友人挑选承载邯郸气韵的礼物，这里都如同一个装满"邯郸灵感"的百宝箱。"坊"间流传：一件好文创，胜过千言万语的安利！

"While others sell souvenirs, I sell the soul of the city!" From the moment it opens, Hanbaofang (literally "The Lane of Handan Treasures") exudes this confident charm. Representatives from Handan's 20 districts and counties gather here in friendly competition, offering the very best of local produce, cultural creations, and tourism treasures, both online and offline.

Here, ancient and modern sensibilities blend in delightful harmony: the elegant lines of Cizhou Kiln ceramics now grace warm-toned teaware; the story of Lin Xiangru's humility in Huiche Lane is printed as a slogan on trendy hoodies; and Handan's timeless idioms, passed down for millennia, have been reimagined by designers into whimsical, meaningful figurines and stationery.

Whether you're looking for a unique piece of city memory or the perfect gift infused with Handan's spirit, this is your treasure trove of inspiration. As the saying goes in the "Lane": one great cultural creation is worth a thousand words of recommendation!

02

去邯郸市图书馆与大剧院，仰望城市文化的双子星
Visit the Handan Library and Grand Theater to Gaze up at the Twin Stars of City Culture

图书馆+大剧院+博物馆，联手撑起了市民爱称"大元宝"的邯郸文化艺术中心。其独特的外形融合了青铜文化、磁州窑文化、和氏璧文化，犹如一块无瑕的美玉浮于城台之上，因此也被邯郸市民亲切地称为"城台上的美玉"。远远望去，那流畅的曲线设计，大气！

图书馆内高耸的书架林立，如同通往智慧深处的幽径；宽敞明亮的阅览区里，阳光透过巨大的落地窗倾泻而下，温柔地覆盖在专注阅读的身影和泛黄的书页上。

一墙之隔的大剧院，夜幕就是它的高光时刻——歌剧厅里顶级声学让音符跳舞，小剧场里地方戏婉转唱响邯郸味，先锋话剧台词直戳时代热点。

这两座建筑，一静一动，一藏一显，如同城市文化的双翼，共同守护着邯郸的文脉。

The library, grand theater, and museum together form the Handan Cultural and Art Center, affectionately nicknamed "The Big Ingot" by locals. Its striking architecture blends elements of bronze culture, Cizhou Kiln tradition, and the legacy of the *He Shi Bi* (a legendary jade disk), earning it the endearing local nickname "flawless jade atop the city platform." From afar, the building's flowing curves radiate grandeur.

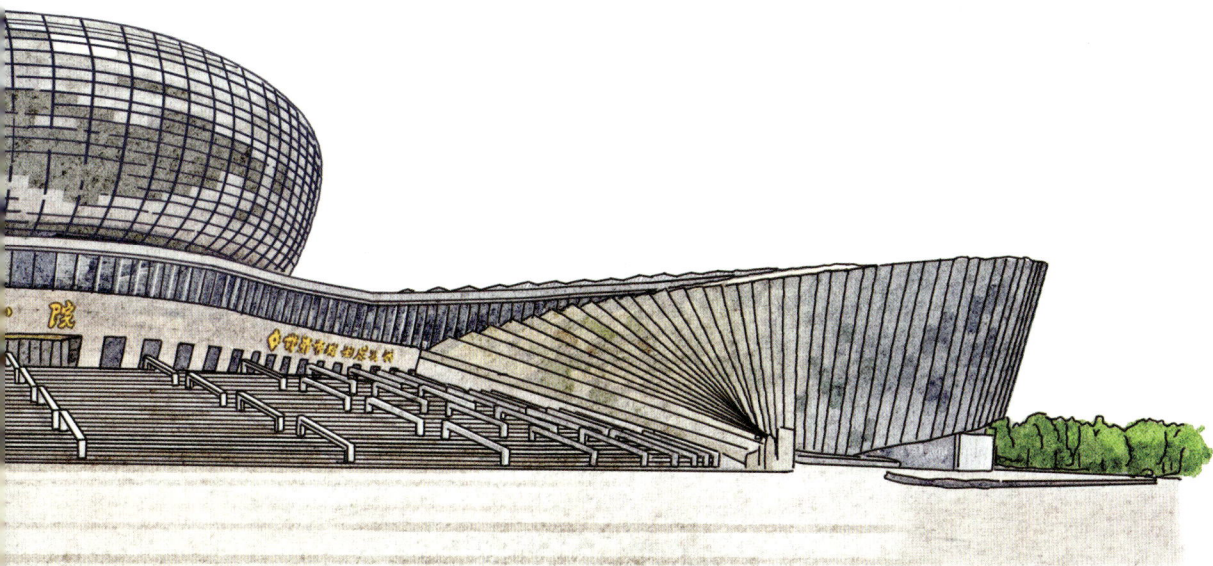

Inside the library, towering bookshelves rise like a forest, forming quiet pathways that lead deep into the heart of wisdom. In the spacious, sunlit reading area, golden light spills through massive floor-to-ceiling windows, gently draping over readers lost in thought and the timeworn pages they turn.

Just next door, the grand theater comes alive after dark. Its opera hall features world-class acoustics that make music dance; its smaller stages host regional opera steeped in Handan flavor; and its experimental theater dares to tackle today's hottest social issues.

One still, one dynamic; one hidden, one revealed—these two landmarks are the wings of Handan's cultural heritage, preserving its spirit while letting it soar.

逛成语一条街，转角遇春秋
Stroll Idiom Street and Turn a Corner into the Spring and Autumn Period

想边逛街边学成语？丛台区光明大街的成语一条街，安排！这条街是邯郸市以成语文化为主题打造的特色街区，全长5.6公里，抬首望去，108个成语灯箱在跨街廊架上向远方延伸，有的还配有AR动画和语音讲解功能；低头可见，105个带有浮雕成语图案的井盖点缀着之前死板的沥青，让冰冷的马路拥有文化的活力；37个成语条石坐凳，让行人们在休憩的同时，领悟成语的深意。

墙壁间、地砖上，乃至店铺的招牌里，都是源自邯郸或与之息息相关的成语典故："邯郸学步"处有诙谐脚印指引方向，"黄粱一梦"旁飘散着米香，"纸上谈兵"边是生意火爆的文具店。商铺也多以成语文化为灵感，售卖相关文创、书籍或提供特色体验。游人穿行其间，目光所及，指尖所触，皆是千年语言智慧的"压缩包"。这条街，让抽象的成语"活"在了路上，逛一逛，便是上了一堂妙趣横生的"行走的成语课"。

Want to shop and learn idioms at the same time? Idiom Street on Guangming Street in Congtai District has you covered! This 5.6-kilometer-long themed street is a cultural landmark built entirely around the rich world of Chinese idioms. Look up, and you will see 108 illuminated idiom lightboxes stretching far into the distance across overhead corridors. Some are even equipped with AR animations and audio explanations to bring the stories behind the idioms to life. Look down, and you will spot 105 intricately embossed manhole covers featuring idiom designs, transforming the once-dull asphalt into a vibrant cultural tapestry. Take a break on one of the 37 stone benches engraved with classic idioms, each one offering not just a place to rest, but a chance to reflect on the deeper meanings behind these age-old expressions.

On walls, floor tiles, even store signs, you'll find idioms that originated in or are closely tied to Handan: "Learning to Walk in Handan" is marked by playful footprints; the scent of rice drifts from "A Dream of Golden

Millet"; and beside "Talking Tactics on Paper," a bustling stationery shop invites exploration. Many businesses here draw inspiration from idioms, selling related cultural goods, books, or hosting themed experiences. Wandering this street, every sight and touch is a "compressed package" of ancient linguistic wisdom. It makes abstract idioms come alive beneath your feet. Every stroll is a captivating walking lesson in Chinese expression.

04

探访中国农业大学曲周实验站，见证科技兴农的神奇魔法

Visit the Quzhou Experimental Station of China Agricultural University, Witnessing the Magic of Technology-Driven Farming

别被"实验站"三个字唬住！这里是现实版"开心农场"和"农业黑科技体验营"！

自20世纪70年代起，中国农业大学的科学家们就在这里扎根，上演了一场现实版"盐碱地变吨粮田"的逆袭大戏。走进基地，就能看到高大上的智能温室里作物享受着"顶流待遇"，还能了解如何用科技手段让土地更"高产"、更"绿色"、更"智慧"。还可以亲手参与一次无土栽培，或是观摩土壤改良的神奇过程，分分钟明白什么叫"科技赋能农业"。

这里把"面朝黄土背朝天"升级成了智慧农业的科幻大片，是大小朋友解锁"舌尖未来"的沉浸式课堂，适合所有对土地和"饭碗"有好奇心的大小朋友！

Don't let the name "experimental station" fool you. This is a real-life version of Happy Farm meets "agricultural tech wonderland"!

Since the 1970s, scientists from China Agricultural University have made this their home base, transforming salt-alkali land into grain-producing fields in a story straight out of science fiction. Inside the station, you'll see high-tech greenhouses where crops enjoy VIP treatment, and learn how technology boosts land productivity, sustainability, and intelligence. You can even try hands-on hydroponic farming or watch the incredible soil improvement process unfold. Within minutes, you'll understand the true meaning of "empowering agriculture with technology."

Here, the age-old image of farmers "facing the loess with their backs to the sky" has evolved into a dazzling sci-fi vision of smart agriculture. It's an immersive classroom for curious minds of all ages who want to explore the future of food and farming.

05

来棉三时光公园，在老厂房骨架里邂逅一场"废墟美学"
Step Into Miansan Time Park to Discover the Aesthetic of Industrial Ruins

当轰鸣的纺织机声远去，老厂房迎来了华丽转身！棉三时光公园，是工业遗产"逆龄生长"的完美典范。高大的锯齿形厂房、斑驳的红砖墙、粗犷的钢结构骨架被完整保留下来，全新的文艺血液却注入其中：咖啡馆飘香，画廊展示着先锋艺术，独立设计师店铺藏着个性好物，创意工作室里灵感迸发，合空间前是一对对拍婚纱照的年轻情侣。

历史与现代在这里无缝交融，硬核工业风邂逅了小资情调，碰撞出独特的"废墟美学"魅力。来这里，点一杯咖啡，在旧时光的齿轮光影里，拍一组质感满满的复古工业风大片，或者只是静静感受一座城市产业变迁的脉动，都别有一番滋味。这里是散养的艺术家们的"精神自留地"，无关年龄，只关风月。

As the roar of textile machines faded, the old factory was reborn in style. Miansan Time Park is a textbook case of "reverse aging" for industrial heritage. The towering sawtooth-roofed plant, weathered red-brick walls, and rugged steel framework have all been preserved, but now pulse with new artistic energy: the scent of coffee fills the air, galleries showcase cutting-edge art, independent designer boutiques offer creative gems, and studios buzz with ideas. Outside the Hé Space, young couples pose for wedding shoots among the industrial relics.

History and modernity blend seamlessly here. Raw industrial aesthetics collide with a refined, artistic atmosphere, creating the unique charm of "ruin beauty." Grab a coffee, shoot a retro-style photo amid the gears of time, or simply soak in the rhythm of an evolving city industry—it all has its own flavor. This is a free-spirited haven for artists and dreamers. Age doesn't matter here, only inspiration does.

06

奔赴鲲乐湾，一键开启狂欢模式
Head to Kunle Bay, Just with One Click to Party Mode

从邯郸市区出发，一脚油门四十分钟，就能遇见"鲲乐湾"。作为邯郸市文旅项目的革新力作、全国首家太阳能光热+文旅综合体示范项目，这里可谓是邯郸一处充满欢乐与活力的大型室内外综合度假区。

全年恒温的"梦幻水世界+雪世界"，简直不要太贴心。逛累了还有温泉酒店，下沉广场能血拼，连停车场都有充电桩。关键是特环保，每年省超多电，玩得开心还不踩碳。无论是追求刺激的"冒险家"，还是喜欢悠闲泡汤的"养生派"，或是带娃放电的"超级爸妈"，都能在这里找到专属的快乐频道，"玩、乐、购、吃、住"一站式搞定！

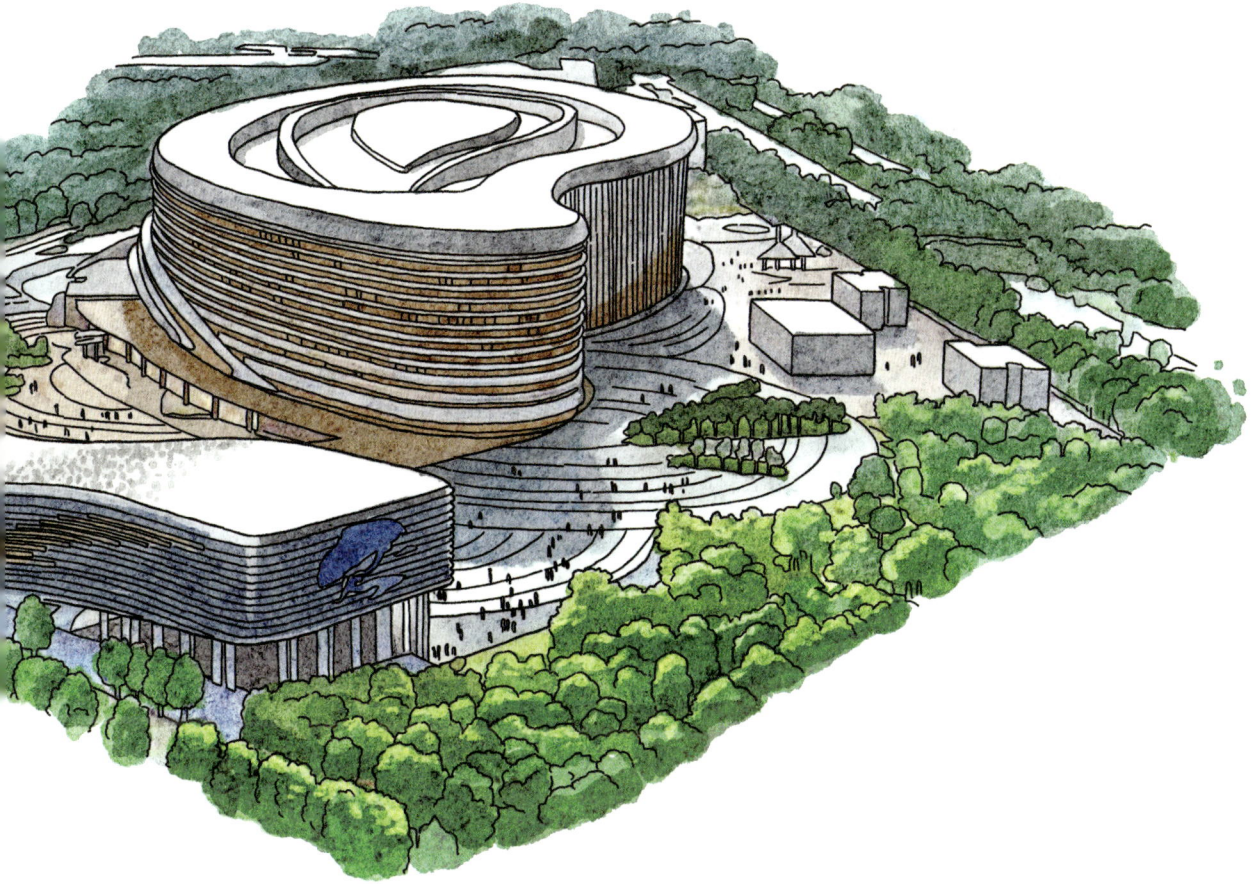

Just a 40-minute drive from downtown Handan, you'll find Kunle Bay, a thrilling new cultural tourism destination and the first solar thermal-powered tourism complex in China. It's a vibrant, joy-filled indoor-outdoor resort and a flagship achievement for Handan's culture-tourism innovation.

Its year-round "Dream Water World + Snow World" combo couldn't be more considerate. Tired from the fun? Relax in the hot spring hotel. Want to shop? Hit the sunken plaza. Need to charge your car? Even the parking lot has charging stations. Best of all, it's ultra eco-friendly—saving vast amounts of electricity annually, so you can play hard without leaving a carbon footprint. Whether you're a thrill-seeking adventurer, a wellness-loving spa-goer, or a super parent looking to keep the kids happy, there's something for everyone here. With entertainment, shopping, dining, and accommodation all in one, Kunle Bay delivers happiness, zero stress required!

07

磁县中华慈大街 18 号 · No. 18 Zhonghuaci Street, Cixian County

畅玩方特国色春秋，在欢腾与惊呼中速成成语典故达人

Dive into Fantawild Legend Kingdom, Mastering Classical Idioms Through Thrills and Cheers

　　成语在方特"活"了！这是全国首个以成语文化为核心主题的大型高科技主题乐园。它将众多源于邯郸或与邯郸历史相关的成语典故，如"黄粱一梦""负荆请罪""胡服骑射""女娲补天"等，通过顶尖的声光电技术、大型机械装置、沉浸式剧场和互动体验项目，变成了可感、可玩、可惊声尖叫的奇幻冒险！坐飞龙在天体验"一飞冲天"的刺激，

在轨道动感小车里见证"女娲补天"的壮阔，让课本里枯燥的文字变成一场场身临其境的狂欢。妈妈再也不用担心语文成绩了！

At Fantawild, idioms come to life! This is the first large-scale high-tech theme park in China with idiom culture as its central theme. Drawing on idioms rooted in Handan or related to the history of the State of Zhao, such as "A Dream of Golden Millet," "Carrying Thorned Brambles to Apologize," "Wearing *hufu* and Practicing Mounted Archery," and "Nüwa Mends the Sky." The park transforms them into fantastical adventures that you can feel, play with, and scream through, thanks to cutting-edge audiovisual technology, towering mechanical installations, immersive theaters, and hands-on interactive experiences. "Soar into the Sky in One Flight" with Flying Dragon Ascending, feel your heart race in a dynamic ride through the epic of "Nüwa Mends the Sky," and watch dry textbook phrases explode into breathtaking, hands-on experiences. With this, moms need not worry about Chinese class scores anymore!

08

游磁州水墨园，穿行在中式美学的"活体"水墨长卷里

Wander Through the Cizhou Ink Garden to Step Into a Living Scroll of Chinese Aesthetics

中国是瓷器的故乡，瓷器是中国的代名词，除了景德镇，民窑顶流磁州窑也必须拥有姓名！

磁州水墨园是以磁州窑文化为核心，以中国古典艺术为载体的艺术园林。建造者巧妙地将磁州窑最具代表性的"白地黑花"艺术精髓融入造园理念。园内以黑白灰为主色调，粉墙黛瓦，飞檐翘角，亭台楼阁错落有致。假山叠石如笔走龙蛇，水系蜿蜒似墨染宣纸。

徽派建筑古色古香，既有湖光山色、烟波浩渺的气势，又有江南水乡小桥流水的诗韵，兼具"北国雄风、情景江南"的意境。

　　穿上华服，执一柄团扇，在黛瓦粉墙间当一回画中人，让磁州窑的千年美学为你一键美颜！

China birthed porcelain, and porcelain defines China. Beyond Jingdezhen, the renowned folk kiln Cizhou Kiln also rightfully claims the spotlight!

The Cizhou Ink Garden is an artful landscape centered on the brilliance of Cizhou Kiln culture and grounded in the forms of classical Chinese art. The designer masterfully integrates the signature style of Cizhou Kiln, black painting on white ground, into its landscape design. The entire garden follows a refined monochrome palette of black, white, and gray: pastel walls, dark-tiled roofs, elegant pavilions, and tiered towers scattered harmoniously throughout. Artificial hills curl like brushstrokes in calligraphy, and winding water systems resemble ink flowing across Xuan paper. The Huizhou-style architecture exudes antique charm, blending the vast, misty beauty of northern lakes and mountains with the poetic grace of southern water towns. It evokes the grandeur of the north and the emotional lyricism of the south.

Put on traditional Chinese attire, take a round fan in hand, and wander among the black tiles and pastel walls. You'll feel like a figure stepping straight out of a painting, with the thousand-year aesthetics of Cizhou Kiln beautifying your every moment.

丛台区光明北大街 103 号 · No. 103 North Guangming Street, Congtai District

09

去成语之都旗舰店，把"智慧梗"打包带回家
Visit the Capital of Idioms Flagship Store to Take Home a Gift of Wit

想带走邯郸的"文化身份证"？成语之都文创旗舰店，就是最生动有趣的实体窗口！

一脚踏进这家店，眼睛先被前厅勾住——设计感满满的空间里，成语文创摆得超有格调，还会跟着节气、节日变花样换布景，春天来是"邯郸学步"的绿意，中秋说不定就飘着"胡服骑射"的古风，每次来都像拆盲盒。里头还藏着好多成语小惊喜：八大类文创市集里，文具、家居、饰品都带着成语的巧思；主题区像场美学对话，走着走着就掉进沉浸式的成语世界里。更妙的是能亲手玩——摸陶土、染丝绢、挥笔墨。

从"邯郸学步"创意冰箱贴到"完璧归赵"艺术摆件，成语文化悄然融入生活细节，每一件小物，都是对邯郸文化基因的趣味解读。挑件心水的"成语"伴手礼，让邯郸故事在你家继续连载！

邯郸 HANDAN

赴汤蹈火　旷日持久
前事不忘
名重泰山　奉公守法
九鼎　前车之鉴
围魏救赵　锲而不舍
相逢　完璧归赵　安如磐石
大吕
广　刎颈之交
路不拾遗
里
之国　浩如烟海　负荆请罪
脱颖而出　邯郸学步
按兵不动　废寝忘食
毛遂自荐
开源节流

成语之都
文创旗舰店

Looking for Handan's "cultural ID card"? The flagship store of the Capital of Idioms is your most vivid and engaging portal!

Step through the door and you're greeted by a stylishly designed front hall: idiom-themed cultural creations arranged with flair, and ever-changing displays that reflect the seasons and festivals. In spring, you'll find the green hues of "Learning to Walk in Handan"; come Mid-Autumn, the scene might shift to a classical wind from "Wearing hufu and Practicing Mounted Archery." Each visit feels like unboxing a new surprise. Hidden throughout the space are idiom-inspired gems: in the eight themed market sections, stationery, homewares, and accessories all brim with idiomatic ingenuity. Themed zones unfold like aesthetic dialogues. You might find yourself unexpectedly immersed in the world of idioms. Even better, you can get hands-on: mold clay, dye silk, or wield a brush to paint.

From creative "Learning to Walk in Handan" fridge magnets to exquisite "Returning the Jade Intact to Zhao" art sculptures, idiom culture subtly infuses daily life here. Every little item is a playful decoding of Handan's cultural DNA. Pick up your favorite idiom-themed souvenir, and let the story of Handan continue in your home!

10

品一杯优布劳，为邯郸的精酿之光干杯
Toast with Urbrew to Raise a Glass to Handan's Craft Brew Glory

啤酒爱好者注意！这里不是单纯的啤酒厂，而是精酿啤酒的"梦工厂"和"文化秀场"——优布劳文化产业示范基地。

走进这里，浓郁的麦芽香气扑面而来。可以透过玻璃幕墙，亲眼见证一粒粒麦芽如何经过糖化、煮沸、发酵、过滤等神奇工序，最终蜕变成杯中那金黄诱人、泡沫丰富的液体"黄金"。基地内通常设有现代化的啤酒吧，提供最新鲜的扎啤和丰富多样的精酿品类，从经典德式小麦到创新果味精酿，应有尽有。还能了解精酿文化知识，甚至体验亲手制作啤酒的乐趣。

来优布劳，现打精酿配德式餐盘！在钢铁丛林的齿轮间，与老友新朋碰个杯——三秒前刚下线的鲜啤嗞嗞冒泡，地道西餐香气撞上纯粹麦芽香，此刻才懂：喝的是烟火气，聚的是真性情。

Attention, beer lovers! This isn't just a brewery. It's a dream factory and a cultural showcase for craft beer. Welcome to the Urbrew Cultural Industry Demonstration Base.

Step inside, and the rich scent of malt hits you at once. Through glass walls, you can watch the magical transformation: malt grains undergo mashing, boiling, fermentation, filtration, and finally become that golden, foamy "liquid gold" in your glass. The base typically features a sleek beer bar offering fresh draft and a wide selection of craft styles, from classic German wheat to creative fruit-forward brews. Here, you can dive into the knowledge of craft beer culture, or even try your hand at brewing yourself.

At Urbrew, order a freshly tapped pint and pair it with a classic German platter! Amidst the cogs of this urban jungle, raise your glass with old friends and new—fresh beer, tapped just seconds ago, bubbles with life. The aroma of Western cuisine meets the purity of malt, and you suddenly understand: you're drinking in vitality and toasting true camaraderie.

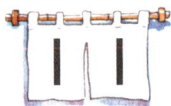

邱县育新北街 8 号·No. 8 Yuxin North Street, Qiuxian County

去邱县青蛙漫画博物馆，用漫画为平凡生活"加梗"

Visit the Qiuxian County Frog Comic Museum to Inject Humor into Everyday Life

　　谁说幽默只属于城市？邱县的青蛙漫画博物馆，是泥土里蹦出的"快乐庄稼"！"青蛙漫画组"成立于1983年，到现在已经四十多个年头了，这里的画家一手握锄头，一手执画笔，把田间趣事、乡村新貌、家长里短，统统画成让人捧腹又戳心的"农民幽默画"，从盼望粮食丰产的《大丰收》，到治沙植绿的《荒漠新影》，从廉政警示漫画《走正道上去的干部》，到精准扶贫乡村振兴的《壮举》，简单笔触下，是农村生活、时代印记最生动的呈现。

　　展览馆里，一幅幅充满乡土气息和犀利观察的作品，分分钟承包你的笑点与泪点。带走一本漫画集，收获的不只是欢乐，更是中国新农村最鲜活生动的"表情包"。

　　Who says humor belongs only to cities? The Frog Comic Museum in Qiuxian County is rural joy bursting out of the soil, a true "harvest of happiness"! Formed in 1983, the Frog Comic Group has been going strong for more than 40 years. Here, the artists hold a hoe in one hand and a paintbrush in the other, turning farm anecdotes, changing village life, and family tales into side-splitting, heartwarming "peasant humor comics." From *Bountiful Harvest* celebrating grain surpluses, to *New Scenes in the Desert* showing reforestation efforts, from the anti-corruption warning *Upright Cadres* to *the Feat* which reflects targeted poverty alleviation, their simple brushstrokes vividly document the era's imprint on rural life.

　　Inside the exhibition hall, every rustic yet insightful artwork is ready to make you laugh one moment and cry the next. Take home a comic book. It's more than joy; it's a colorful emoji pack of China's rural revitalization.

12

到邯郸市体育中心，感受刚柔并济的澎湃心跳
Feel the Pulse of Tai Chi Power at the Handan Sports Center

看！邯郸城东新地标来啦——邯郸市体育中心直接把"太极哲学"穿在了身上！罩棚透光带巧妙扭成优雅双螺旋，仿佛阴阳流转的现代演绎。走进场馆更是惊喜连连：蓝白座椅拼出太极星云图案，与头顶的螺旋钢棚遥相呼应，在这儿运动，莫名有种行云流水的畅快感。

邯郸市体育中心可不是只会"搞大事"的家伙！三万观众席摆开，不管是盛大的开幕式、激烈的田径赛，还是热血的橄榄球对决，都能稳稳"拿捏"。但更圈粉的是它的亲民属

性——全民健身、演唱会嗨唱、展会市集……统统接得住！从专业运动员到遛娃家庭，都能找到属于自己的主场。

Look! A new landmark has risen in eastern Handan—the Handan Sports Center, literally dressed in Tai Chi philosophy! The transparent roof canopy spirals into a graceful double helix, a modern homage to the flow of yin and yang. Step inside and discover surprise after surprise: the blue-and-white seats are arranged in a Tai Chi nebula pattern, mirroring the spiraling steel canopy above. Exercising here feels like moving through flowing clouds—effortless and exhilarating.

With 30,000 seats, it confidently hosts grand opening ceremonies, intense track and field competitions, or adrenaline-filled rugby showdowns. But don't be fooled—it's not just for big events. What truly wins hearts is its inclusivity—open to the public for fitness activities, concerts, expos, and local markets. From elite athletes to families with kids, everyone can find their own home turf here.

13

栖居溢泉湖，在"天鹅湖"畔贩卖落日与浪漫
Retreat to Yiquan Lake Where Sunset by the "Swan Lake" Meets Lakeside Romance

邯郸的刚毅里藏着一颗柔情明珠！镶嵌于磁县怀抱的溢泉湖，是一座兼具防洪、供水、灌溉、发电、养殖与旅游功能的大型水利枢纽。

冬日，成千上万只野生大天鹅翩然而至，溢泉湖瞬间化身梦幻"水上芭蕾剧院"。租辆单车环湖漫游，看水鸟掠过金色芦苇；乘一叶轻舟摇曳碧波，任湖风温柔拂面；待到夕阳熔金，霞光染红水面与天鹅剪影，随手定格都是大片。这里是摄影师的"天堂滤镜"，情侣的"浪漫充电站"，更是都市人短暂出逃的诗意和远方。

Beneath Handan's rugged exterior lies a tender, shimmering gem. Embraced by Cixian County, Yiquan Lake is a vast hydraulic complex serving flood control, water supply, irrigation, power generation, aquaculture, and tourism.

In winter, tens of thousands of wild swans descend gracefully upon its waters, transforming Yiquan Lake into a dreamlike "ballet theater on water." Rent a bike for a lakeside ride and watch waterfowl soar over golden reeds. Drift across the rippling surface in a small boat and feel the breeze kiss your face. As the sun melts into gold and silhouettes of swans ripple across the reddened water, every snapshot becomes a cinematic masterpiece. It's a natural "photo filter" for photographers, a romantic "recharge station" for couples, and a poetic getaway for city dwellers in need of beauty and breath.

去磁州窑艺术馆，在千年窑火中"陶"醉
Visit the Cizhou Kiln Art Museum and Get "Pottery-Enchantment" on a Millennium of Fire and Clay

　　磁州窑的千年星火，在此生生不息！这座国内规模最大的磁州窑主题艺术馆，由一级工艺美术大师、非遗传承人安际衡先生创办，堪称一座活的陶瓷"基因宝库"。馆内完整保留了拉坯、修坯、刻花、剔花等古法制瓷流程，更集宋元古瓷的朴拙遗珍与当代大师的创新力作于一身——行走其间，仿佛在触摸一部立体的中国陶瓷史诗！

　　在安际衡等非遗传承人的守护下，磁州窑艺术馆巧妙融合传统与当代：既严格遵循古法，又以创新设计焕活经典。例如，将香薰孔嵌入瓷枕，让千年技艺飘出时尚芬芳，轻松圈粉年轻一代！

更妙的是，游客还能亲手"玩泥巴"！在导师指导下体验拉坯、刻画、上釉的乐趣，无论艺术发烧友还是亲子体验派，都能在此找到与泥土对话的纯粹快乐。

The thousand-year flame of the Cizhou Kiln burns on, undying and vibrant! Founded by master artisan and national intangible cultural heritage bearer An Jiheng, this is the largest Cizhou Kiln-themed art museum in China, a living "genetic archive" of ceramic artistry. Within its walls, the full process of traditional porcelain-making is preserved in detail: wheel-throwing, trimming, carving, and incising. The museum brings together both rustic relics of Song- and Yuan-dynasty ceramics and innovative masterpieces by contemporary artists. Walking through the space feels like touching a three-dimensional epic of Chinese porcelain.

Under the guardianship of An Jiheng and other masters of intangible heritage, the Cizhou Kiln Art Museum weaves tradition and modernity into a seamless tapestry: it strictly follows ancient methods while infusing them with fresh, creative design. For example, ceramic pillows are now embedded with aroma diffuser holes, allowing thousand-year-old craftsmanship to exude a modern fragrance that easily captivates the younger generation!

Even better, visitors can get their hands dirty with clay themselves! Guided by skilled instructors, guests can experience the joy of wheel-throwing, engraving, and glazing. Whether you're an art enthusiast or a family looking for a meaningful outing, you'll find pure delight here in your dialogue with the earth.

15

丛台区滏东大街与油漆厂路交叉口东行 300 米路北 · 300 meters east of the intersection of Fudong Street and Youqichang Road, north side of the road, Congtai District

沉浸在左之书店，在书页的密林里构筑一方精神原乡

Lose Yourself in Zuozhi Bookstore Where Thick Pages Build Your Spiritual Homeland

北京有单向空间，上海有钟书阁，成都有方所……邯郸，有左之书店！

推开左之书店的门，喧嚣瞬间被按下了静音键。这里不是连锁书店的复刻，而是邯郸独有的"知识盲盒"与"灵感发酵池"。进入书店大门，首先看到的就是邯郸本地文史书籍。店内装饰也反映了很多巧思：书店办公室门的镂空灵感源于磁州窑"梅瓶"；书店办公室"莲花顶"灵感则来源于邺城文化遗址的柱础。书店名字"左之"更是取自《诗经·小雅》："左之左之，君子宜之"，为这座精神粮仓平添了许多"文艺范儿"。

在这家复合式书店，可以读名著、看文章、听音乐、品咖啡，还可以经常参加文化活动，如作家讲座、读者交流会等，让思想的火花在此碰撞。

Beijing has OWSpace, Shanghai has Zhongshuge, Chengdu has Fang Suo Commune… and Handan has Zuozhi Bookstore!

Step through the doors of Zuozhi Bookstore, and the bustle of the outside world fades into a hush. This is no cookie-cutter bookstore chain, but Handan's own "knowledge blind box" and "fermentation pool of inspiration." The first thing you'll see is a collection of local books on Handan's history and culture. The interior design is full of thoughtful details: the carved office door draws inspiration from a Cizhou Kiln Meiping vase, and the "lotus dome" ceiling of the office echoes the column bases found at the Yecheng cultural site. Even the name "Zuozhi" is drawn from *The Book of Songs · Minor Odes*: "*Zuozhi, zuozhi, junzi yizhi*" (Go left, go left—the noble man goes forth with ease), lending a distinct artsy vibe to this cultural granary.

This is a hybrid bookstore where you can read classics, browse essays, listen to music, sip coffee, and even join regular cultural events like author talks and reader meetups. It's a space where ideas spark and minds connect.

16

点一杯弥山咖啡，感受提神醒脑的"成语特调"
Order a Cup of Mishan Idiom-Infused Coffee, Wisdom and Energy in Every Sip

　　在邯郸市博物馆一楼，藏着一座让文化"活"起来的宝藏咖啡店——弥山咖啡！这里不只卖饮品，更是用一杯杯成语创意，讲述邯郸的千年故事。

　　"胡"服骑射鲜奶茶：天山草原鲜奶撞上太行山好茶，一杯喝出草原与农耕文明的激情交融，奶香茶韵，双倍满足；一"茗"惊人纯茶：传统六大茶类精粹，却自带年轻人钟爱

的花果香气，轻松解锁中国茶魅力；奇货可居文创咖啡：咖啡＋邯郸成语＝世上仅此一杯的奇思妙想，干了这杯成语咖啡，苦尽"甘"来！

这里不止饮品独特，杯子更是文化艺术品，身披最具邯郸文化的载体——成语。逛馆累了？快来弥山，解锁一杯能喝、能品、能晒、还能"涨知识"的成语咖啡吧，保证让你爱不释手，晒足朋友圈！

Tucked away on the first floor of the Handan Museum lies a hidden gem where culture comes alive in a cup—Mishan Coffee! This café doesn't just serve drinks. It tells Handan's stories, one idiom at a time.

Try the "Wearing *hufu* and Practicing Mounted Archery" Milk Tea: fresh milk from the Tianshan Mountain grasslands meets fine tea from the Taihang Mountains—an exhilarating fusion of nomadic and agrarian civilizations. Creamy and aromatic, it satisfies on every level. Or savor the "A Sip to Astonish" Pure Tea (a wordplay on the idiom "A Cry That Astonishes the World"): crafted from the finest of China's six traditional tea types, but enhanced with floral and fruity notes beloved by younger palates—a refreshing take on classic Chinese tea culture. Don't miss the "Qihuo Keju" Creative Coffee—where espresso meets idioms. Inspired by the phrase *qihuo keju* ("rare goods are worth hoarding"), it's a one-of-a-kind sip of Handan wit. Take a sip of this punny brew and taste the "Sweetness after Bitterness"—literally and figuratively!

But it's not just about what's in the cup. The cups themselves are cultural works of art, wrapped in idioms that capture the spirit of Handan. Tired after your museum tour? Drop by Mishan to unlock a drink you can taste, savor, show off, and learn from—a cup that's as Instagrammable as it is insightful. Guaranteed to charm your taste buds and light up your social feed!

17

来赵王印象城，感受古赵文化的深厚底蕴
Visit the Zhao King Impression City and Experience the Rich Legacy of Ancient Zhao Culture

　　古赵文明的腹地邯郸广平，一座"活着的赵王城"正散发着醇厚的酒香与历史的回响——这便是赵王印象城，它以"工业+旅游+文化"的创新融合，织就了一幅沉浸式的几千年古赵风情画卷。

　　步入北区，时光在酒香中倒流。五个朝代酒肆林立，古法酿酒技艺在此生生不息。当历史情景剧《鲁酒薄而邯郸围》徐徐展开，一个关于"意外牵连"的故事跃然眼前：鲁国酒味淡薄，与赵国毫无关联，却让赵国都城邯郸无端遭受围困。这一幕不仅展现了邯郸酿酒文化的深厚底蕴，更以其戏剧性的历史典故，令今人深思何为因果。

　　当暮色四合，南区华章奏响。赵王不夜城灯火璀璨，汉唐风韵交织市井烟火，填补了邯郸东部的夜游空白。而印象赵王剧场内，战马嘶鸣，蹄声如雷，《战国风云·平定中山》大型实景马战以惊险特技再现古赵雄风，引人屏息。

In Guangping, Handan, the heartland of ancient Zhao civilization, a "living city of King Zhao" breathes with the mellow fragrance of aged liquor and echoes of history. This is Zhao King Impression City, a place where "industry + tourism + culture" are seamlessly interwoven to create an immersive scroll painting of ancient Zhao life spanning thousands of years.

Step into the northern district, and time seems to flow backward on the scent of spirits. Taverns representing five dynasties line the streets, where traditional brewing techniques continue to thrive. As the historical vignette "Lu Wine Was Weak, Yet Handan Was Besieged" unfolds, a story of unintended consequences comes vividly to life: though the State of Lu's wine was bland and seemingly unrelated to Zhao, it inexplicably led to the siege of Handan, capital of the State of Zhao. This dramatized episode not only showcases Handan's rich heritage in winemaking, but also prompts reflection on the ripple effects of cause and consequence.

As dusk falls, the southern district lights up in brilliant splendor. The Zhao King Sleepless City dazzles with lights, where Han and Tang-style architecture blends with the buzz of everyday life, filling the void of nighttime attractions in eastern Handan. Inside the Impression Zhao King Theater, warhorses neigh and hooves thunder—the grand live-action equestrian show "Warring States Turmoil: Pacifying Zhongshan" recreates the martial glory of ancient Zhao with breathtaking stunts, leaving audiences breathless.

Sketches of Classic Handan

Written by Wang Fang and Tian Xiao

Illustrated by Xu Xiangyu and Liu Tianyu

Translated by Ma Rui

First English Edition 2025

By China Pictorial Press Co., Ltd.

Address: 33 Chegongzhuang Xilu, Haidian District, Beijing, 100048, China

ISBN 978-7-5146-2582-0